20/01/23

- ∽∂

STEPMOTHE

/

STEPMOTHERING

Donna Smith

 HARVESTER
WHEATSHEAF

New York   London   Toronto   Sydney   Tokyo   Singapore

First published 1990 by
Harvester Wheatsheaf
66 Wood Lane End, Hemel Hempstead
Hertfordshire HP2 4RG

A division of
Simon & Schuster International Group

© Donna Smith 1990

Typeset in 10½/12 pt Bembo
by Photoprint, Torquay

Printed and bound in Great Britain by
Billings and Sons Ltd, Worcester

British Library Cataloguing in Publication Data

Smith, Donna, 1931–
  Stepmothering.
  1. Step–mothers
  I. Title
  306.8'743

ISBN 0–7108–1134–9
ISBN 0–7108–1208–6 pbk

---

1 2 3 4 5   94 93 92 91 90

To my mother and father

Contents

Acknowledgements

I am deeply grateful to:

Erica De'Ath, whose idea it was to write this book.

The stepmothers who talked or wrote to me and shared their experiences with me. They were an endless source of inspiration.

My husband, who was patient and encouraging throughout the project.

The National Stepfamily Association, especially the founders, Dick and Elizabeth Hodder.

Many friends, but especially Jane Batchelor, who let me talk to them when my confidence flagged.

My sons and my stepson, who continue to teach me about themselves.

And, most of all, to Linda Masters, who was the first person to read the manuscript and who gave me ideas, suggestions and enormous help.

An open letter to a stepmother

During the many months I worked on this book, most especially in the first phase when I was interviewing stepmothers, one thought returned again and again, often in the middle of the night. That thought, really two questions, was: What do women need to know when they become stepmothers? What would have been helpful to me to know, right from the beginning? I decided that whatever else would be included, some answer to those questions must be attempted, and I would assume, perhaps arrogantly, that an answer to the second would help to answer the first. This is a letter about what I think would have been helpful to me twenty-nine years ago. It is largely about what I did not know.

I did not know that I would feel in competition with my stepson for his father's time and attention. I did not know that I would become fiercely protective of my own two children when they struggled with a new authority figure and were compelled to compete for my time and attention with my husband and stepson. I did not know that as we forged the pattern of our daily lives, each one of us – children and adults – had a different set of expectations based on our previous daily-life patterns. Also, each one of us had a different combination of needs for affection and understanding. We did not talk about all the different needs and expectations. I believe that had we simply talked about how things 'used to be', sadness and also angry feelings would have dissipated more quickly and we would have been taking care of each other in an affectionate way. But we were frightened that talking about the past would upset our new and fragile connections.

Contacts with my former husband were a reminder of a past I was trying to ignore. Because contacts with him were stressful in the beginning, I assumed they always would be. Now I know time helps to reduce stress, and does so more quickly if the past is accepted. I also know that my children suffered, having to absorb tensions we adults should have dealt with ourselves.

We all knew a great deal about living, down to the youngest. In an indirect fashion we did share what we knew through our daily lives. We were active, we did things together, but our varied pasts, with all that we had learned from them, were taboo as far as direct references were concerned. I think we were frightened about being different from one another. Two of us, my husband and stepson, knew a great deal about dying and the loss of a loved person, for my husband's first wife had died after a long illness. That terrible and rich experience was closed off, too intimate and too painful to be part of our new family.

What was a new beginning for me and my husband, full of hope and joy and optimism, was a frightening experience and a kind of ending for our combined children. It sounds trite to say that being 'in love' made us blind to the children's struggles. I well remember seeing my stepson walk away from us the day we married, sullen and baffled. I can see his young stiff back, his cap and plaid shirt. I realised how he was feeling, but I did not know what to do about it. I comforted myself with a naïve belief that I could overcome his misery. My two sons had not lost their mother, nor their father either, because he was living and they had contact with him. But they did not know what to expect of the new situation and another huge change in their lives. There were aspects of the new life which pleased each of the children, and these helped. The certainty which my partner and I felt, the warm and active approval of our wider family, carried us through the upheavals which followed, but we could have done it better. I do not mean to imply that we could have avoided upheavals, but we were not prepared for them. Each new crisis produced more guilt, especially in me.

How could we have done it better? Suppose I had followed my stepson when he walked away from us that day and had talked to him, about – about anything – in an effort to let him know I was not stealing his father and did not want to obliterate the memory of his mother. He needed to remember her and talk about her. As time went on, the subject of his mother became ever more difficult to broach; it was too painful to be mentioned. Suppose his father and I had said to each other, 'This must not happen; we must ease this, for him and for all of us. We must use the past to enrich our present, rather than be threatened by it and pretend the family we have now is the family we have always had.'

Suppose we had been more open about our previous family lives and more accepting of being different – from one another and different as a family from other families? I know that I tried to pretend that differences did not exist. I felt they were an indication of failure on my part, failure to create a 'normal' loving family. When I think about how I might have handled things better, had I not been trying so hard to squash us into a mould we did not fit, I remember incidents like this one: we were all at a restaurant when the waitress complimented me on my children and said they all looked like me. I smiled at my stepson and saw his angry distress. He did not say, 'She is not my mother!', but it was written in his expression. I had been feeling it was rather a good secret joke, a mark of success in the pretence of being an 'ordinary family' until I saw his face. What I wish I had done – and could have done had I had a different definition of myself and of our special family – was to say, 'That's rather funny because we are a stepfamily and this is my stepson. I'm proud you think he looks like me, but he actually looks like his own mother'. That would have been a message of respect not only to my stepson and his loyalty to his mother, but also a message to my own children that their security and right of place in our family did not require them to live a double life. They could love their own father and also love and grow in our new life, a life of great joy and satisfaction to them in many ways. When I realised that the children, especially my stepson, were resisting the game of pretence, I thought I was failing in my job of being 'mother' to all of them. Rejection breeds rejection, so as I interpreted my stepson's anger and confusion as rejection of me, I began to reject him, and to fear that my husband would, in turn, reject me and our marriage. Had I known that my stepson did not need me to replace his mother, but something different, our whole relationship would have been clearer from the start, not the murky thing it was for several years. I do not mean to say that it would have been free from conflict and turbulence, but that it would have been free from damaging pretence and rumbling, suppressed anger. I believe that had I held an ideal of pioneering a kind of family life which contained several families and created its own history every day, and had my husband and I shared that kind of ideal openly and talked about how best to make it work, I would not have suffered grinding self-doubt and imagined that I was failing. I am sure I would not have made the mistake I did make in creating more and more distance between all three children and their other parents – living and dead.

As I have explored the issues involved in stepmothering, read the findings of research and examined images of stepmothers in literature, I have discovered that my ignorance is not unusual nor my experience exceptional. I have also discovered that stepmothers are still under pressure to conform to the model of 'just an ordinary mother' and that this is the model held up by many people who give advice to stepmothers struggling with their situation. My hope is that this book will provide you with some alternative models. I hope, too, that those who are not stepmothers will find the book useful and come to understand something of what it means to be a stepmother.

With all best wishes,

DS

Introduction

This is a book about stepmothers, about who they are, the many and various ways in which a woman might become a stepmother, about how they are represented in folk tales and literature, about what society expects of them and, most of all, it is about what they expect of themselves. I spoke to, or communicated with, more than thirty stepmothers and their answers to my questions are recorded here. In addition, I examined my own experience as a stepmother and compared it with that of the stepmothers I interviewed and with the studies about stepfamilies and stepmothers which I read. Although there is also reference in the book to family therapy and to my work as a family therapist, this book is not about my professional or personal experience. Those factors merely form part of the framework for discussing stepmothering and understanding what the stepmothers themselves said.

In the time it took to carry out interviews, review them, think about what women were saying to me about themselves and their lives and put that into a context of cultural expectations with an historical perspective, my ideas and aims clarified. And this process of clarification largely took place as I listened to the voices I had recorded on tape and typed up their words. Putting the book together was rather like weaving; the warp of personal statement and the woof of background information meshed and each gave strength and meaning to the other. The background material includes sociological information on the effect of parental loss and the development of what society expects of mothers. I have tried to describe and elucidate the cultural message about stepmothers by tracing the history of stepmothering through a selection of writers' work, some popular, some obscure. And, in order to illuminate some of the interview material, I have also included one or two clinical studies of women who suffer stress and depression in their role as stepmother.

1

Now, as in the past, stepmothers have to contend with the image of the 'wicked stepmother'. I have examined its source in folk and fairy tales and outlined the consistent representation of the stepmother as a character of cruelty and malice. One of my principle aims in writing the book was to liberate stepmothers from their 'wicked' fairy tale image. Stepmothers, and women in general, also have to contend with the myth of the 'perfect mother', which led me to propose a choice for stepmothers. Stepmothers need not be threatened by the myth of the perfect mother; they can choose to be other things to their stepchildren, not a mother figure, but a friend, a confidante, or a sponsoring adult, perhaps. The choice can be determined by a particular stepmother in a particular family in terms of the needs of the child and her ability to provide for those needs. Women do make many choices for themselves in contemporary life, for example, to pursue a career and remain independent, or to have a partner but not a child, or to have a child and also a career. Yet often, a woman who has courageously made choices for herself feels bound and confined by conventional expectations when she becomes a stepmother. It is as if the cultural messages about the 'wicked stepmother' leave her no option but to attempt to overcome the negative expectations.

The context of stepmothering is the family, and the family is affected by the wider context in which it exists – society. There is a great deal of social approval for the nuclear family of two parents and children but less for other family forms, and perhaps only tolerance at best. Such is the dilemma of the stepfamily, and its individual members may experience more or less discomfort as a result, either in the small private family context or the larger, public social context, or both. Stepmothers occupy an uncomfortable position in society, the very word 'stepmother' carrying connotations of evil, and within the family the stepmother is viewed with suspicion, in the early stages certainly, by the children and possibly the extended family also. She cannot be anything but in the wrong when she enters their lives. Add to the confusions for her the fact that she has an intense emotional investment in being successful because of her attachment to her partner, and you have a situation sometimes referred to as a 'double-bind' (Bateson, 1973). The stepmother wants to create a strong family context for the sake of her partner and his children; she needs the children's acceptance in order to achieve her goal and she needs support from outside the family, social approval, in her role. She lacks this, and usually the more the children reject her the less social support she receives. It takes time, much adaptation and compromise, and also imagination, to overcome the stresses.

Many children experience the divorce of their parents and, of course, there is much concern about how they are affected, and specifically, how they are affected by the possible loss of a parent. On the other hand, a number of children have always been at risk of losing a parent but through death, not separation and divorce. In past times only the very wealthy were able to end an unhappy marriage through divorce. Today about one third of all marriages, it is estimated, will end in divorce. Many children will acquire stepparents while both their parents are still living, and they are more likely to live with a mother and stepfather than a father and stepmother. One study of stepchildren found only 11.6 per cent lived with a stepmother, (Knaub and Hanna, 1984), but many of the others had a stepmother in the home which they visited when in contact with their father. Why be concerned about stepmothers when most of them are not living full time with their stepchildren? The answer lies in the numbers of stepmothers who apply for help to agencies and counsellors. Part-time stepmothering can sometimes be more difficult and stressful than full-time; the role of the part-time stepmother is extremely ambiguous. How does she fulfil her role? Is she needed at all? As more is learnt about children's need to maintain contact with both their parents after a divorce or separation, more thought needs to be given as to how stepmothers can be advised and helped to cope with all the situations in which they can find themselves.

A number of assumptions about roles and relationships within families are still firmly held in spite of the fact that, 'There is now no single British family but a rich variety of forms, states, traditions, norms and usages' (Laslett, in Rapoport *et al.*, eds, 1982, p. xii). For example, it is assumed that women are financially dependent upon men, that women care for children and are responsible for the emotional life of all members of the family. Stepmothers are disadvantaged by such assumptions in at least two important ways: most stepmothers are in paid employment as a matter of necessity and they are not linked emotionally to the children in the same way a mother is. Two-thirds of all married women are in paid work (Parker, in Rapoport *et al.*, eds, 1982) and one study of stepfamilies found over 70 per cent of the women employed (Knaub *et al.*, 1984). Many stepmothers will be following a career, and job satisfaction is especially important to stepmothers whose self-esteem suffers as a result of difficulties in fulfilling their stepmother role. The assumption that it is the woman who cares for the children in the family and looks after their emotional needs can contribute to a stepmother's loss of self-esteem, for it is impossible for her to function as if she were the natural mother when she lacks an intimate knowledge of the children and they do not accept her.

Despite the fact that these assumptions are unrealistic at the emotional and psychological level, they are backed up by social policies which disadvantage stepmothers, for example in relation to the taxation of married women. It is assumed that the husband is the wage earner, but many stepmothers provide a major and vital portion of the economic support of the family, especially if the husband is paying a percentage of his income for the maintenance of his children and their mother's home. A child-care policy which gave choice to working mothers and did not also take stepmothers into account would be unfair to them. Many stepmothers must remain in paid work to help support the family and, in addition, also look after their stepchildren. Obviously full-time stepmothers, those whose stepchildren live with them, will be caring for children and in many cases, working outside the home as well. What is less obvious is that part-time stepmothers, carrying financial responsibilities and perhaps pursuing a career, often see more of their stepchildren than is expected and look after them for long periods. Some even become full-time stepmothers when children change residence, a situation which can happen suddenly and be unanticipated.

The fact that there is no legal relationship between step-mothers and stepchildren contributes to their social and cultural ambiguity. Laws which affect the family do not acknowledge the importance of steprelations in either married or cohabiting families. Although divorce is sanctioned, families which form following divorce have a dubious social status. Many of them try to disguise their stepfamily structure and appear 'normal'. For both adults and children this is usually unsuccessful and unhelpful. Children are loyal to their first family and their two parents; adults are frustrated, depressed and dismayed by attempting to fit a model which they did not grow into.

PART I

The stepmother and society

CHAPTER ONE

The making of a stepmother

An enormous amount of giving is required – more than the heart may hold.

A stepmother

Stepmothers have existed in human life for as long as we can know. Mothers die and a substitute has to be found; a father needs help in caring for children and a home, and he falls in love with another woman who tries to fill all the roles her predecessor filled. Couples separate and form new partnerships and stepfamilies are created. Whether there is a legal remarriage or not is of little significance to children whose father is living with someone other than their mother, and we shall see that a legal marriage does little to enhance the status of stepmothers. In this book any woman who lives either full time or part time with her partner's children will be referred to as 'stepmother'.

The very word, stepmother, is an ancient, unlovely word, loaded with connotations which are the opposite of the one it is inextricably tied to – mother – and this is true in languages other than English. In Spanish, for example, there are many soft and endearing words for mother: *Madre, Mama, Mamita, Mamaita, Madrecita, Mamasita*, and one harsh word for stepmother – *Madrastra*. The Spanish friend who told me this said the word sounds like 'someone very big will come and eat you. You have to think of the connotations the word has from Cinderella and stories like that.' Indeed you do, and every child grows up knowing them. The French word for stepmother is the same as the word for mother-in-law: *belle-mère*. It has a pleasing sound and translation to English is also pleasing, for it means beautiful mother. However, its usage is not kind, as both mother-in-law and stepmother are seen in a derogatory light. The French trait for diplomacy, in language as in manners, disguises a distaste

9

for both roles, making *belle-mère* an ironic term. It carries the same connotations as does stepmother in English and evokes the same images from fairy stories.

The unlovely words, stepmother, and stepmothering, will be repeated over and over in these pages. Whether the sound will become more or less welcome remains to be seen. When my small granddaughter wanted to capture my attention one day, she tried various ploys, then hit upon this: 'I know what', she said, 'I'll be a prince, and you be a princess, and I'll take you around the world on my horse!' Of course I was entranced, and I said, 'O that's wonderful! What shall we see?' She was thoughtful. Finally she answered, 'We're going to see a lot of the horse.' It is unavoidable, isn't it? You are riding a horse and you see more of it than anything else. In a book about stepmothering there are no substitutes for the words 'step-mother' and 'stepmothering' and no way to avoid their frequent use.

The beginning for a stepmother follows upon the end of a chapter for a first family. Whether a mother has died or parents have separated, it will be stressful for a child, tragic in the case of death or total loss of contact. Today, much concern is voiced about the rising divorce rate and the effects of divorce on children. There is talk of 'the breakdown of the family'. Stepmothers seem to personify these fears. One stepmother put it this way:

> **'Some people are embarrassed when I mention that I am a stepparent. It has connotations of failure (divorce), being second best (second wife), and it is a challenge to the myth of the "happy family". People either tend not to want to know, or to want to know all the intimate details.'**

There is great difficulty in establishing a way to present oneself to a world which is uneasy about stepmothers.

Perhaps most of us long for a time we imagine to have existed when there was greater stability and certainty, when marriages did not end and when a wide network of extended family provided security and help when it was needed. Today's isolated nuclear family of parents and children is sometimes cited as a cause of the high divorce rate, and the extended family is held up as a lost ideal. Historical sociologists tell us, however, not only that the nuclear family has been the norm for three hundred years, with most households consisting of only two generations; they also tell us that losing at least one parent in early childhood has always been a common experience. Wherever records exist this fact of life in previous generations is evident (Laslett, 1977). There is a tendency to 'look on our own generation as burdened by the problem to an extent never paralleled in the past' (*ibid.* p. 161), and we pity ourselves and our children. But if we compare twentieth-century figures for children with parental deprivation with those from the nineteenth century and earlier, there is a remarkable similarity.

In America today, where divorce and remarriage are commoner than in other countries, some 12–15 per cent of children aged 17 and under have lost contact with a parent because of separation and divorce. We can assume this to be the highest rate of parentally deprived children at present (*ibid.*). In Britain, Rimmer (1981) estimated that between 16 and 20 per cent of children under 16 are likely to see their parents divorce. To reach a probable figure for parentally deprived children – those who have lost a parent – we should divide those percentages by half. We know that many children lose contact with one parent within two or three years following separation (Law Commission, 1986) and some estimates are that as many as half do. Thus it is possible that in current British society as many as 10 per cent of children under 16 have lost a parent. But in pre-industrial England the number of children who had lost either mother or father or both was likely to have been significantly higher. For example, a study of the population of Bristol in the late seventeenth century concludes that one child in three had lost one or both parents, certainly a higher percentage than for parental loss due to divorce (Laslett, 1977, footnote, p. 169). Taking figures available for various places in the West during the eighteenth century, a third of children had lost parents, one or both, and 21 per cent before the age of 9. Children in our time are not disadvantaged by parental loss in such numbers. According to Laslett's surveys, the very highest percentage of children under 18 who have lost a parent is a little over 16 per cent:

> It cannot be said that parental deprivation is commoner under the conditions of the late twentieth century in high industrial society than it was in the seventeenth and eighteenth centuries in traditional

society. It looks as if the reverse might be true. We are hardly justified, in historical terms, in sympathising with ourselves for the prevalence of broken marriages in our time and its deplorable effects on our children. (*ibid*. p. 170)

It seems that parents have never been able to promise to stay alive or to stay married for the whole of their children's early life.

In previous generations, however, death was far more likely to be the reason a child lost a parent than parental separation and divorce. Children may be losing parents at a comparable rate in contemporary society, but most of those parents continue to live. What is new for children is having a parent who is alive, but lives elsewhere, and having other, additional adult figures in daily contact, in a parent's place. What is new for stepmothers is having to create a meaningful relationship with a child whose mother may be, and probably is, active in the child's life. What then, *is* the stepmother? Obviously, she is not a replacement mother. In fact, even if a mother has died, a replacement is not appropriate under all circumstances – for adolescents and young adults, for example. They need adult guidance and friendship but not the degree of nurturing and physical care a small child needs.

There is discussion in the helping professions as to whether it is more difficult to be a stepmother following death or following divorce, and many believe, as many stepmothers also believe, that death creates a clearer context. It is easy to imagine that a stepmother has a less complex and ambiguous task when the mother has died. But in either situation the child remains loyal to the mother, if only to her memory; the stepmother cannot replace or displace her. When a mother dies she will usually become an idealised figure, especially if the child is old enough to have vivid memories of her. It is possible for a fantasy to develop about how she would always have been a perfect mother – always understanding, forgiving and loving. The stepmother has to compete with this idealised memory. You cannot negotiate with a ghost; you can only try to help a child to resolve grief. A living mother can have a similar and equally powerful influence on the life of a stepmother, creating seemingly insurmountable problems, but the possibility to resolve them exists.

How do we account for the long-standing image of the wicked stepmother and its extraordinary power and prevalence? Even today's authors, whose stories and articles are almost always about stepmothering following divorce, not death, use the fairy tale figures as touchstones when discussing the themes we are setting out to explore now. For example, in the May, 1986 issue of *Everywoman*, there is Sheilagh Jevons' article, 'Stepmother scapegoat: Snow White syndrome and the dilemmas of stepparenting', or 'Cinderella revisited' in *The Invisible Web*, a case discussion by Olga Silverstein, family therapist (Walters, *et al.*, 1988). There are many other examples. Stepmothers I talked to referred again and again to the fairy stories and their influence.

Many lives are affected by all this, although it is difficult to obtain accurate figures. There are some safe generalities. In spite of the fact that stepmothers are numerous and familiar in folk tales, in real life there are fewer stepmothers than stepfathers. In earlier times, as now, children were more likely to lose father than mother, whether through death or divorce, and losing both parents, it seems, has always been rare. There are no accurate figures for how many stepmothers there are, or how many children have stepmothers. Children are more likely to remain with the mother following divorce, and we know that the divorce rate has increased since the early 1960s with a dramatic rise after the change in the divorce law in 1969. It was a few more years before the divorce rate overtook the death rate as the primary reason for marital dissolutions. We know that the divorce rate is high, but that the remarriage rate also is high: one in three marriages is a remarriage for one or both partners (Rimmer, 1981). Obviously many thousands of children are affected by these remarriages. We also know that many couples maintain a stable relationship without a legal ceremony and that children are involved in both types of re-formed families, some as full-time members of the household, and some as children visiting their non-custodial parent, returning, probably to mother, after visits. Therefore, there are many women who are stepmothers on a part-time basis, the most common form of stepmothering today, and their numbers are impossible to assess. Many of their stories and comments and understandings will appear in this book. Like the full-time stepmother, they have to struggle with issues of fitting into pre-existing families, feeling excluded, and not knowing how to 'mother' a child who already has a mother.

Children who live all or part of the time with father and stepmother, whether their own mother is living or not, will have experienced a disruption of contact with the parent they are almost always most intimately dependent upon, the mother. The stepmother is a symbol of that disruption. That is her ancient, timeless position. There, in 'mother's shoes', she personifies the basic fear of childhood, the loss of love and certainty.

Indeed, if we examine definitions, we find the very word, 'step', means loss; it comes from Old English 'steop' and Old High German words linked with those for bereaved or bereavement. If you have a stepmother, you have mother-loss, total or partial, in terms of the ideal we hold of an ever-present mother. Perhaps for children to have lost their first family constellation, where parents were clearly fixed, visible, defined, and predictable, is a 'kind of death' for which the grieving never quite ends; at least, one stepmother put it that way, and she speaks as a stepchild as well as a stepmother. It takes a lot of work to help children, of all ages, overcome such loss. Most stepmothers have to put up with having their attempts to help rebuffed again and again, and with being seen as the negative stereotypic stepmother.

Even the dictionary definitions present an unrelenting picture of the abusing, neglectful figure. Webster's *Collegiate Dictionary* (1948 edition) gives a first simple definition: 'Stepmother: the wife of one's father by a subsequent marriage', but in a later and longer edition (1961), examples are provided in order to show usage: 'one who fails to give proper care and attention'. The *Shorter Oxford English Dictionary* (1973) gives this example: 'Said of a bird that hatches another bird's eggs'. (Many stepmothers told me they somehow felt they were 'stealing' another woman's child if they succeeded in establishing trust and affection.) The Oxford dictionary shows how the noun becomes a verb, 'to stepmother': 'to provide with a stepmother, especially with suggestions of unfairness or cruelty'. Funk and Wagnall's *New Standard Dictionary of the English Language* (1949 edition) provides an ironic folk definition. It says that a hangnail, that irritating and sometimes painful bit of flesh which hangs at the root of a fingernail, is a 'stepmother's blessing'. The *Dictionary of Slang and Unconventional English* (ed. Beale, 1984) tells us that expressions such as 'step off' and 'step out' refer to dying, confirming the link between the word 'step' and death. The *Scottish National Dictionary* gives the Scottish for stepmother: 'step-minnie' – and tells us that in Scotland a year of death or privation is known as a 'stepmother year'.

No wonder women shrink at the very mention of the word; it carries terrible suggestions of the feelings most feared, not only by stepmothers, but by mothers themselves. A woman who was not a stepmother said to me, 'When I am impatient and irritable with my children and resent their demands, I feel like a stepmother to them.' A mother's greatest failure is to be 'like a stepmother'. A friend of mine joined households with a man whose two adolescent children were living with him – their mother lived abroad. When I said to my friend, 'So now you are a stepmother', she recoiled. 'That sounds so awful, I'm not that.' What is she then? There is no doubt that my friend is in a stepmother role, and seeking her own way to interpret its meaning, while finding its connotations difficult to bear.

We have no other word in common usage which covers the relationship between a child and the woman who is the father's partner but not the child's mother. In today's family there is no simple description or definition. A woman may have the care of her partner's children on a full-time basis with all the physical and nurturing care falling to her, and probably most of the disciplining also. This is the situation, familiar over the centuries, which occurred because of the mother's death. It might now occur because of a custody arrangement which makes the father the custodial parent following divorce from the mother. It is unusual, but it does happen, and is becoming less rare. It might also happen that the mother has custody of the children, but they spend half or more than half their time with the father and his new partner, the stepmother. She will then be living with the children and trying to find a suitable role with them for a big portion of all their lives. I talked with women who stepmother in these and other ways.

The most common form of stepmothering in contemporary Western society is the part-time form; the children live with their mother but spend weekends and holidays with their father and stepmother, because of the usual custody arrangements which follow divorce. Since men tend to remarry more quickly than women, within two to three years on average (Ihinger-Tallman and Pasley, 1987), we can assume that many children whose parents have separated or divorced will acquire a stepmother within that time. Part-time stepmothers do become full-time ones when children move from mother's home to father's, and this happens, although records of custody awards suggest otherwise. Under a pending change in law relating to families, custody and access will become redundant concepts: children will reside with one parent but have contact with both. That children have a right to and need the involvement of both their parents is emphasised by the principles of the Children Bill 1988, due to be implemented in 1991. Stepparents, although not named in the bill, must have a role in actively supporting the involvement of a partner with children from a previous family. Since it is in most cases the father who is the 'contact' parent, stepmothers are frequently in the position of facilitating such contact. However, a woman who marries or lives with a man who has children may not realise that she will become a stepmother in any sense, or be aware of her significance in helping father and children to remain connected. Many women I talked to had expected to play little or no role with visiting stepchildren and certainly had not been prepared for the complexities of the relationship. They also often said that neither biological parent seemed to be aware of or concerned about the stepmother's problems in relating to the children.

Stepmothers whose stepchildren are adults when the step-relationship begins also face problems. Of all women who married in 1980, just over 50 per cent married a divorced man while 6 per cent married widowers (Kiernan, 1983). The average age of the women who married widowers was 46 and a reasonable assumption might be that any children would be young adults not directly involved in the new marriage. That assumption was belied by the women whom I spoke to in that category; they were surprised to find they were expected to assume responsibilities for the emotional and psychological care, and sometimes the physical care as well, of people in their twenties and even thirties. Even when adult children live away from the parental home, they can make unexpected demands on the older generation and sometimes harbour feelings of great bitterness. When a father remarries or forms a new partnership, adult children may feel dispossessed of their inheritance, they may feel their parent is behaving inappropriately for his age in forming a new alliance, or that their mother is being negated by it, or they may simply resent the presence of a new person with their familiar parent. Older children's loyalty to the first family can be challenged just as much as young children's. Relationships with children of any age alter when the parent forms a new partnership. A woman who is now herself a stepmother reflected upon her own experience of acquiring a stepmother:

> **'My father married again when I was 19. I never saw him on my own again. She was always there, and I resented it very much. I think she must have known how much I resented it, and was probably afraid of what I would say about her.'**

That woman is now in her late forties and became a stepmother to two people in their twenties. She expected them to resent her and they did. She is sure that because she was prepared she was less distressed by her stepchildren's initial hostility than she might have been and was able to take decisions about alleviating it. For example, she made sure that her stepchildren continued to have periods of time with their father when she was not present. Knowing what to expect in stepfamily life does not prevent it happening, but knowledge is a great aid to survival.

Here is another voice: 'When I was in my early twenties my father remarried. From then on I always had to negotiate with this intruder in order to see my father.' Even though both her father and stepmother are now dead and twenty years have passed, this woman speaks with anger and sadness. Her stepmother might have described the situation in very different terms. She might have felt her stepdaughter's hatred, and when you feel another person's hatred, when you feel that your very existence is resented, you begin to hate back, and then it seems all the myths of wicked stepmothers have come to live in yourself. It is especially painful for a woman in the role of 'mother' to admit either that she arouses hatred in a child or harbours such feelings herself. The traditional role for a woman is that of mother, a mother who is loving whatever her circumstances. The antithesis of this role is the rejecting stepmother. Stepmothers, no matter how old their stepchildren, have to try to love and accept them as they would their own children, while simultaneously coping with feelings of being resented.

It is generally agreed by researchers, clinicians, and other writers (Burgoyne and Clark, 1984) that there is a high level of stress involved in being a stepparent, and that the stress is greater for stepmothers than for stepfathers because of the expectations placed on the female role in families. Stepfathers have problems similar to those of stepmothers – being resented by the children, rejected as a disciplinarian, excluded from the parent–child relationship which preceded the new partnership and so on – but do not suffer the same degree of distress or loss of self-worth (Morrison and Thompson-Guppy, 1985). Women are still expected to take primary responsibility for the emotional and psychological health of the family, as well as the major burden of child care. Men are expected to carry the major burden of financial support for the family. These traditional expectations may conform less and less to the actual experience of men and women as more women work outside the home. Only about 5 per cent of households actually conform to the traditional model of the nuclear family with a woman at home with the children and a man the single breadwinner (General Household Survey, 1982). Yet, the cultural expectation is that women will care for the family emotionally, whatever the family constellation. This plainly does not fit the stepfamily, where the children may not even be known to the stepmother, and she may not have chosen to act as their mother; she has chosen a partner. A foster mother, or adoptive mother, has, by contrast, chosen to care for children who are not hers by birth. A woman who becomes a stepmother may or may not be attracted to the children to whose father she is attracted, but she will be drawn into caring for them whether they live with her or not. Her partnership will be affected by the way she responds to her partner's children and she will often feel helpless and ineffective when trying to do what is expected of her. She will have to cope with her own anger at being rejected by the child – 'for a long time he just ignored me as if I wasn't there, and of course that was what he wanted, for me not to be there' – and she may also feel rejected by her partner when there is family tension, tension which she feels it is her job to dispel.

In public most stepmothers try to act as a mother, do what a mother does, while in private they can experience enormous stress and loneliness. This applies in all stepmothering situations: full-time, with children living in the stepmother's home and maintaining no contact with their mother; full-time, with children living with stepmother and visiting mother; part-time, with children living with mother and visiting father and stepmother's home; part-time, with children living with mother but spending half or more time with father and stepmother; part-time with children having free and unspecified access to both homes; and the situation in which a woman maintains her own home, but spends a great deal of time with her partner and his children, either in her home or his. Three of the thirty women I talked with are stepmothers in this last-mentioned situation. They struggle with the same issues, feel left out of the intimacy when the children are present, feel confused and angry and overburdened at times, but also have affection for the children they are helping to raise to adulthood. I have been impressed with the sensitivity stepmothers show for the feelings of their stepchildren even when they are feeling excluded and unhappy themselves. One woman, who has children of her own, who does not live with her partner but has his children to stay every weekend and sometimes for longer periods, talked about her concern that her stepchildren might become confused about where they belong, or feel they were being disloyal to their mother if they enjoyed being with her, the stepmother. She worried that all the children, her own and her stepchildren, might feel forced to betray the important adults in their lives because the adults require such different things from the children. She knows that by being caring and loving with her stepchildren she fuels their mother's fears that she will 'poach the children's affection', in effect, 'steal them'. This is a stepfamily of more than usual complexity, but while showing her sensitivity and her concern for all the children, this woman also acknowledged her jealousy of her stepchildren who had a prior claim on their father, and her occasional feelings of loneliness and confusion. This is how she put it:

'There is an element of truth in the stereotypes. You can become the wicked stepmother because of the competitiveness between yourself and the children. The children can become symbolic of competition for their father. I never feel that way about my own children. They are always individuals to me, and I know what I am to them, and what they are to me.'

The private experience of being a stepmother is often one of confusion, ambiguity and self-doubt. A woman who has experience as a mother to her own children can still feel inadequate when trying to relate to stepchildren. Most stepmothers go through a period of disillusion also, when they realise that they will not automatically love the child or children of the man they have fallen in love with. When they become aware of their negative feelings they feel ashamed and fearful that the new partnership will fail as a result. For women who have no children of their own and are stepmothers on a part-time basis, there is a particular kind of ambiguity; the public expectation exists, yet they have no maternal 'rights' and no access to a mother role. There seems virtually no purpose for them in relation to the children. They often feel barely tolerated and severely excluded from the relationship between the father and his children. No role seems to work; obviously, the 'mother role' is inappropriate. As this stepmother described it:

'If you are a non-custodial stepmother and you have no children of your own, it is a situation of enormous invisibility. People don't believe or take seriously your involvement with the children. No value, it seems, is attached to what you contribute or to anything else you know. It's a kind of cheek to call yourself a stepmother – a poaching on other people's territory. You truly are an outsider. In the early stages I [had feelings of hatred toward the children] and I felt ashamed of the hatred in myself. I did not want the children to be hurt by it. I used to go off until I could control the hatred better. I felt everyone hated me. I felt mean! But as time goes by I have learned that I don't need to invest so much. There isn't a clear parental kind of role, but there also is not the primary responsibility for the children. They have two very good parents already. I can enjoy them, and get something back from them, especially as they get older. I can have closeness and fun without the whole burden. But it is muddling and difficult to get the balance right. What are you? A friend – not a mother – but not nothing. I am not afraid of losing the children, but afraid that they don't really need me in their lives. I rarely go to

them but I wait for them to come to me; I wait for their
overtures. They don't come out of love as they do to their
father, but because I am a friend. I take their part sometimes.'

Another stepmother, also part-time, said:

'When you say the child comes on weekends and school
holidays it sounds like such a neat package. Doesn't describe the
thing at all! Imagine – all over the country there are children
travelling around to different homes. . . . And whatever you
do, the children and stepmother have no legal bond.'

As the two women quoted above say, in the privacy of the
family stepmothering is a powerful emotional experience, but in
public the stepmother is either invisible – she goes unrecognised
– or is expected to take on a mother's responsibilities,
sometimes to the extent of pretending the steprelationship does
not exist.

Many stepmothers, those with marital status as well as those
without, say that outsiders encourage them to pass themselves
off as the child's mother; they also say that they can see
embarrassment in people when the steprelationship is mentioned. There is no legal status for stepmothers or stepfathers in
English law, no kind of public sanctioning. It is as if society has
decided to sanction the ending of an unworkable marriage, but
remains very uneasy about stepfamilies (Visher, 1984). The
ideal model of family life which gains approval is still that of
two parents and their children. Divorced families, families
headed by one parent and stepfamilies have one thing in
common – they do not conform to the accepted model. It is
hardly surprising, therefore, that stepfamilies often try to
conceal their steprelationships. A study done in Sheffield by
Burgoyne and Clark (1984) showed that many stepfamilies do
try to 'pass as normal'. Some of my interviews also bear this
out. Pretending the steprelationships do not exist usually adds
to the tensions and seldom succeeds, for obvious reasons: the
children remember their other parent, treasuring the memory of
a parent who has died or feeling loyalty towards a living parent
with whom they may have little or no contact. Feelings in a
stepfamily are different from those in a traditional family,
histories and therefore memories are different, the loyalties are
complex, and the wider family network is not common to all
members.

Burgoyne and Clark studied a group of stepfamilies which had come together when the children were very young. In their typology of stepfamilies (Table 6.1, p. 194) this group is titled 'not really a stepfamily' because these families saw themselves as approximating closely to society's norm and the distinction, 'stepfamily', seemed irrelevant to them. There were few issues which concerned them, for example, contact with former spouses, and it may be worth noting that in most of these families the stepparent was stepfather, not stepmother. The stepfather had assumed a role with the children when they were small and they had a minimal relationship with their own father. These families did not try to hide their stepfamily status, but they had little cause to expose it. As the children grow older they may want to explore their parentage and may challenge the 'ordinary family' myth, and this can add a further dimension to adolescent turbulence. One stepfamily I met in the course of clinical work showed signs of the tension which can arise when a stepfamily is unable to discuss family relationships openly. Adolescent children from the mother's first marriage had known their stepfather almost from infancy and obviously had a warm relationship with him. However, when I asked the most simple questions about their history, there was an obvious heightening of tension in the family. The smaller children made more noise, the older children became more active in controlling them and the parents showed anger at having to respond to my questions. While I do not think that being a stepfamily was the central issue for them, or at the root of the problem which had brought us together, it obviously was a source of strain affecting all the family and to some extent a factor influencing the way they dealt with family problems. It was not an open subject. It was too threatening to their sense of being 'normal' and, therefore, acceptable.

Burgoyne and Clark write:

[There is a] paradox which lies at the core of investigations into the nature of steprelationships. In societies where the nuclear family is regarded as an ideal – the natural, healthy and desirable type of domestic arrangement – family structures which cannot entirely conform to that norm will be regarded and their members may regard themselves, as deviant. In discussions of the public issues involved the attention of researchers, policy-makers and other 'experts' will be focused on the structural ambiguities and aspects of family relationships which distinguish such families most clearly from 'normal' nuclear families. However, when asked, stepparents themselves seem to be at pains to point out their conformity and commitment to nuclear family norms. (p. 25)

Parents want to do their best. If they cannot provide the ideal family – ideal according to the social norms – they want to provide one that is as near as possible to ideal. They do not want their children to grow up in a family which is labelled deviant, or seen as a poor substitute. The pressure to 'pretend' is great. I asked stepmothers if they introduce themselves as such, or explain to outsiders the nature of their family. Their answers reveal the desire to protect the children and the children's loyalty to their own mother, but also the desire to protect themselves from outside scrutiny, while at the same time not exposing the children to unnecessary hurt because they have a non-conforming family. Here are the responses of five stepmothers:

A 'Other people don't always help. Some say, "What a shame for the children." It's a bit like airing your private life in public to explain to casual acquaintances, but if the relationship is going to continue, it must be explained.'

B 'I introduce my stepson by his name, not as my stepson. I don't want him to feel second class.'

A 'You can see people trying to put you into the mother position, sizing you up and evaluating your age, and whether the children look like you. That's when it's easier to say, "I'm their stepmother." If I'm never going to meet them again, I don't bother.'

C 'I don't know how the kids feel about me giving myself the role of stepmother, being a kind of part mother, rather than just doing what is necessary to take care of them. I do know I don't want to explain the situation in front of them, in case they feel something terrible has happened to them in their life.'

D 'It's a hard word, stepmother. Recently one of my stepchildren introduced me to a whole group of her friends in a pub as her stepmother. I felt I wanted the floor to swallow me. I never wanted to be their mother; I just happened to be married to their father. I wanted to know them, be a friend, but a little bit of me was pleased that she acknowledged me in that way.'

C 'The children need an explanation, other people don't, but you just can't find a way to do it. By the time children know what marriage is, it seems simple to tell them that people can have more than one, and what happens to children.'

B 'But by the time children know what marriage is, they know people are not supposed to have more than one. Being a stepmother sometimes feels like taking responsibility for something that is not your mess. I seem to think about it more than anyone in our family, and my stepson comes to me, not his father, to ask questions about what the family means.'
E 'My stepchildren use me that way, too; someone to talk to on the subject of their parents' marriage and divorce. With outsiders I often don't own up to being a stepparent as I don't like being the object of idle curiosity.'

These women are thinking hard about their children and stepchildren, about what is happening to the children in the process of growing up in a stepfamily, and they are sensitive to the children's feelings, however difficult and painful life may be for them as stepmothers. Privately they may feel anger and resentment at having to shoulder the burden of children they did not choose and may have hardly known when they began caring for them, and publicly they cope with a kind of exposure to scrutiny which is not imposed upon the nuclear family.

A stepfamily's desire to appear 'normal' and not be recognised as a stepfamily, or, at the very least, to appear to be succeeding, has a parallel with what some other families which do not conform to the ideal feel, for example, adoptive or foster families, or families with a handicapped child. Margaret Voysey (1975) showed that parents of handicapped children claimed that their family life was very little affected by having such a child. On the other hand, both observable and indirect evidence suggests that having a disabled child does change family relationships and is emotionally and physically extremely difficult. If some parents do acknowledge these difficulties, it is usually later in the life of the family (Hannam, 1975). Voysey suggests that parents with a disabled child will claim that they are managing well and are not greatly affected because they wish to give an account of themselves which corresponds to the images of good and normal parents. She suggests, as does Hannam, that contact with members of helping professions may even add to pressure to live up to the model of 'good parents' and lead them to deny that they have feelings of anger or resentment about the child, or need special help. Professional people carry the same cultural ideals as everyone, and as one stepmother pointed out, can even seem to have a more condemning attitude than 'ordinary folk'. 'If you don't fit the usual expectations,' said another, 'you can feel quite bashed by experts.' So, with outsiders, ordinary folk or experts, families which do not conform to the ideal will present themselves as 'normal' in as many ways as possible.

Adoptive families and foster families may also wish to disguise their differentness. Foster families sometimes change their foster child's surname in order to avoid awkward questions at school, for example. It is current practice to encourage both these family types to be open with their children and, in the case of foster children, to maintain links with their family or origin. Foster families probably have the least difficulty in wearing their identity in public. Foster parents are doing a paid job which they choose to do, and their willingness to take it on shows the world that they have been successful parents. They have been approved by professional examiners, and are highly valued for the work they do. Yet, foster parents, particularly foster mothers, having difficulty controlling a foster child or integrating a child into the family, speak of many of the issues raised by stepmothers, and also adoptive mothers: they want to present a public image of successful parenting, they feel they are being scrutinised and condemned for any 'failure', and their private feelings of guilt and failure make them suffer from low self-esteem, sadness and anxiety.

Although stepmothers are often compared to adoptive and foster mothers, there are important differences which should be made clear. In all three categories the mother is not the biological mother of the child, and to some degree will be acting in place of the mother in terms of caring for the child. The differences lie in the degree of care and in the area of choice. A foster mother chooses to foster children; an adoptive mother chooses to adopt a child; a stepmother chooses the father of the children. A foster mother and a woman who adopts are seeking fulfilment through the care of children. Stepmothers are seeking fulfilment through an adult relationship. Stepchildren may add to the richness of that relationship and a stepmother may find the children an added bonus, indeed she may see herself as creating new hope for the children as well as for herself and her new partner, but that is seldom her primary reason for entering the relationship. One of the most difficult questions that a newly formed stepfamily has to resolve is who comes first in the natural parent's life – the children or the new partner?

In contrast, when a couple adopt, the decision is a joint one, and the child is desired wholeheartedly by both of them; adoption is for life, and the adopted child has the same legal status as one born to the couple. Foster children are not necessarily a permanent part of the family, and may be part of more than one household, just as stepchildren often are. But fostering is a formal arrangement, backed by law, and payment is made for the board and care of the child. Stepmothers have no legal relationship with their stepchildren, whether or not they have legally married the father and, of course, no payment is involved. Both foster mothers and adoptive mothers are viewed with admiration by society while stepmothers are almost always viewed with suspicion. Although a foster mother and a stepmother have in common the fact that the children they care for nearly always remember their biological families and have loyalties to their natural mother, unlike a stepmother a foster mother shares the fostering status with her partner, the foster father. The stepmother, on the other hand, is an outsider to the father's relationship with his child. The adoptive mother, if she adopts a baby or infant, does not have to compete with the child's memories of another mother, but she must still honour the child's birth history and may have to tolerate the child's pursuing his or her biological parents at some stage. There is counselling available to help adoptive families through that stage, and statutory counselling when adoption procedures begin; there is counselling and continuing support for foster families also, which is part of the fostering contract. Stepfamilies do not automatically receive guidance from informed and experienced professionals.

When professional workers become involved with a stepfamily it is often because there are unsettled issues left over from the previous family, and for no other reason. No assumption exists that stepfamilies need guidance for themselves and little agreement exists at this time as to what guidance there should be. Therefore, professional workers usually represent a negative and stigmatising experience for the stepfamily and are a reminder of a painful past, undermining their efforts to make a new beginning. Even stepfamilies who seek guidance may find little available to them because awareness and knowledge of stepfamily issues based on research and compared over many stepfamilies and over time is still scant. There is, however, the National Stepfamily Association (see Appendix 1).

Stepmothering and being a foster mother or an adoptive mother are fundamentally different activities with few, if any, areas in common. Consider, for example, a stepmother's feelings towards a child, adolescent, or young person, whose relationship with her begins before her relationship with her partner has had time to reach the stage of adding children. Time for the couple to develop trust and intimacy is limited and much of it is shared with the children. The children are there from the beginning and the couple have no time to plan how they will assume responsibility for them, whereas a foster mother makes careful plans, usually with a partner, about caring for a child, as does an adoptive mother. The basis is quite different in each case, of course. The foster mother agrees to care for, house and feed a child, but can opt out. (However, foster children are frequently loved by their foster mothers and sometimes spend their entire childhood and adolescence in one foster family.) The adoptive mother assumes she will love and care for her child as if it were her own, although things do not always go well and some adoptions break down. The point I am making is that stepmothers have no choice about taking on their partner's children; they have no preparation period, no time to test the parenting partnership and they seldom share their hidden anxieties for fear of seeming to reject their partner. Above all, they are unclear about what it means to be a stepmother. What should her relationship to her stepchildren be? Is it a good or bad thing to be a stepmother, and for whom? The starting point is that the stepmother is an outsider *vis-à-vis* the father and his children; she was not part of their previous family history. The newly formed couple is the most fragile element in the wider family complex as well as in the small unit of parent, stepparent and children (Visher and Visher, 1979).

There is another woman, the children's mother, who has intimate ties with the children and a claim on the father to continue a parenting partnership. There may be emotional ties between the two parents, of either friendship or bitterness, which intrude upon the closeness and privacy of the new couple. If the mother has died, her ways of doing things, her rules and wishes may still be very much alive in the children's minds, and they may be mourning her. She is 'there', whether spoken of or not.

In legal terms, the stepmother does not exist. Stepparents have no legal status and, therefore, no legal parental rights, although as adults they do have certain obligations towards stepchildren, such as seeing that they are properly cared for, educated and are not abused (Stacpoole, 1988). In general, rights and responsibilities are contingent upon one another in law, but steprelations are an exception, since stepparents are expected to assume the usual responsibilities of parenting and family life without enjoying any of the rights of parents. This means that a stepmother who cares for a stepchild either all of the time or part of the time has no right to apply to have the child live with her should the father die or should her partnership with him end. On the other hand, if she has been legally married to the father and becomes divorced from him, has treated her stepchild as a child of her family, and the child requires financial maintenance, she might be required to pay it (*ibid.*). It would be extremely unusual for a stepmother to be ordered to pay maintenance on behalf of her stepchild, but the fact that she could be highlights the peculiar legal position of stepmothers, and of stepfamilies in general.

A stepmother can become the legal mother of her stepchild – be named on the child's birth certificate, have all the duties, rights and responsibilities of a parent – through an adoption order. This means that the father and stepmother together adopt his child, effectively cancelling out the mother in legal terms, and the courts now have a duty under the law to consider whether this is really in the child's best interests. There are other ways to protect children and to establish a degree of legal connection with stepparents. For example, stepchildren do not inherit by right from a stepparent, but making a will which names them gives them status equal to other heirs, their stepbrothers and sisters, or half-brothers and sisters. Also, a parent can appoint a legal guardian of his or her children; this can be a wife or husband who is the stepparent, and who in this way acquires certain legal rights over the children. If there has been no legal marriage with the stepparent this is difficult to do, as is custodianship or wardship, both of which give certain legal ties. The new Children Bill, due to be implemented in 1991, may provide a certain element of security for stepchildren and stepparent bonds should the stepfamily end. It provides for categories of persons other than parents who are close to the child, so that an important relationship can be maintained. An order providing for contact can be made (Section 7 orders) and older children can themselves apply for contact with someone they might otherwise lose. It is still ambiguous, however, reflecting ambiguity in social attitudes towards stepfamilies.

And yet, in spite of little or no legal status and negative social images, stepmothers are now, and always have been, of enormous importance in the lives of children. Society depends upon them to care for children who would otherwise be motherless, and to act as mothers to children whose parents are divorced or separated. At the same time they are often presented as a curse. In much literature they are portrayed with bitterness, sorrow and misunderstanding. If you ask young children what a stepmother is most will tell you it is a 'witch' or someone who is wicked. Stepmothers do occasionally appear in literature as idealised models of selflessness, the ideal of motherhood itself. Both images are unhelpful to women living the day-to-day life of a stepmother, privately trying to make things right for children they may hardly know, whose mother they may hardly know, if at all, but who nonetheless exerts a powerful influence on their lives, and at the same time trying to appear in public as a competent 'mother'. Many stepmothers feel their partner does not support them or understand their personal stress. They may be able and confident in other aspects of their lives yet feel a failure as a stepmother. They are unlikely to have any positive models to draw upon for either their private efforts or public appearances and possibly little or no support or encouragement from the wider family.

In a nineteenth-century novel with a title every stepmother can identify with – *The Young Stepmother: A chronicle of mistakes* (C. M. Yonge, 1861) – the family of the central character speaks of her intention to marry a widower: 'but to see her at three-and-twenty, with her sweet face and high spirits, give herself away to a man who looks but half alive, and. . .have the charge of a tribe of children, be spied and commented on by the first wife's relations.' And here are the words of a stepmother in 1987:

> 'My mother was thrilled for me when I told her I was going to marry, but her manner changed completely when I told her he had a child. She was wary for me, she wanted me to think about it. It was not the dream she had for my marriage.'

Listen to this stepmother:

> 'It's not that I have felt criticised by other people, but that other people don't think about stepfamilies at all, except for the problem ones. You are just expected to become a mother of some kind, but if you waver, there is enormous condemnation. Often the response to any complaint I make to my friends or my family is, 'Well, you knew he had children when you married him.' When I feel I am doing all right with it, I feel that I am a very special and close friend, not a mother really. It is closer than friend, because it is family, but better than family because there isn't the same obligation or duty involved. It seems freer, with the element of choice there is in friendship. I am partly responsible for [my stepdaughter's] life – but only as much as she wants. With my stepson, nothing works. He expected a cruel stepmother and that's how he sees me. He didn't want his father to marry again.'

And this voice:

> 'Whatever is happening, you feel very alone in it. You are alone in it. I try to be decent and practical and never show the hurt. Is it fair to a woman? It is a tremendous drag on your resources at every level. If you have a lack of confidence. . .you could go under. In the first year you have to give and give and take kicks from the kids and not let your own needs show, even when you feel like an abandoned child yourself.'

When women become stepmothers, they appear to have little choice about the form of stepmothering they are to provide. Their partner and the outside world, rightly or wrongly, generally expect them to take on the role of mother, and stepmothers usually wish that role upon themselves. People fear the worst from a stepmother, and even expect it, but demand the best. Listening to stepmothers, hearing how emotionally drained they often are, considering the ambiguities of their social position, the pressures upon them to succeed, their own expectations of themselves and their fears of failure, all set against the cruel stepmother myths, makes me wonder: does every stepmother have to live down the 'wicked stepmother' myth and prove it wrong in her case? Most of the stepmothers I talked to felt tainted by the myth from the start. It takes a huge effort of will to ignore the social images of stepmothering while bearing the initial resentment of children, the exclusion from the affection and attachment between the children and their father, the prior claim of the children's mother and their loyalty to her, and perhaps also the suspicion of grandparents who fear losing their grandchildren. And yet, many stepmothers survive and are grateful for the stepchildren in their lives, just as many children gain from the stepmothers with whom they grow up.

CHAPTER TWO

A short history of stepmothers in folk and fairy tales, mythology and literature

'I would have adored Miles as a stepfather! and fairy-story jokes are about stepmothers anyway, not about stepfathers, – I wonder why?'
Family History, Vita Sackville-West

In plays and novels, in classical mythology and many historical accounts, and always in folk and fairy stories, the stepmother appears as a hated and hateful figure. A woman who becomes a stepmother is acutely aware of the stereotype she will be compared to at some time, either by others or by herself. Every stepmother I contacted spoke of the spectre of the 'wicked stepmother' and of the fear of turning into one, especially at times when her feelings for a stepchild were resentful and negative. She may be prepared for it, but a woman finds the experience of disliking a child, even temporarily, frightening and shocking. The wicked stepmother seems to step out of the pages of the children's books and come to live in one's house.

Fairy stories and folk tales still form the core of children's literature and are familiar to most children. The oldest, best-known folk tales feature stepmothers, and they are, without exception, figures of cruelty. What is more, their cruelty is directed towards children. What could be worse? Folk tales have evolved but the cruel stepmother has not changed, though other features have altered. In fact, stepmothers appear more often in the stories most familiar to us than they once did. Long before folk tales and fairy stories were collected and published as literature for children, they were told over and over, gaining and losing details and emphasis in different times and cultures. In the West today, these stories have stopped evolving and have now taken on forms which are nearly static. Since the first collections of folk tales were published, the stories have been revised to reflect and to convey prevailing values and standards.

Now, in film versions, especially those made by Walt Disney, they are fixed in the form and with the details familiar to us. If the stories are traced back we find that some versions have disappeared, at least in the West; indeed an entire tradition of stories about strong and active women has disappeared, and this fact is relevant to stepmothers and to women generally. As different versions of the tales were published, the ideal men came to be portrayed as aggressive, the ideal women as passive. Aggressive female figures, and those with attributes of jealousy, greed, or vanity, became witches or stepmothers. Stepmothers were used to epitomise what came to be seen as an evil force – assertiveness in women. For example, in earlier versions of one of the most familiar tales, Snow White had a jealous and murderous aunt, not a stepmother (Opie and Opie, 1974). Today, when we think of *The Story of Snow White*, we immediately think of vengeful stepmothers, as we do when we recall the most famous story of all, *Cinderella*, while the characters of the two heroines are synonymous with feminine virtues of service, passivity and beauty. There are male monsters as well as heroes and princes, but of cruel relations, no figure representing them appears more often, or is more famous and infamous, than the stepmother (Thompson, 1946).

The Cinderella story has been powerful in keeping alive the stepmother stigma. It is the universal fairy tale, used without referent to mean abuse, neglect and even ridicule. Every child knows it; its popularity has existed for centuries. It entertains and delights, but folk tales and fairy tales have functions beyond those of providing entertainment and stimulation to the imagination. The stories, with their beauty and magical solutions for impossible dilemmas, also provide frameworks to explain certain natural phenomena and to explain the inexplicable, such as murderous mother figures. And they have an important social and cultural influence, educating children to hold approved values and attitudes. Today the influence of folk tales has increased, not only because of their wide availability, but because they are available in the form and with the emphasis writers have chosen to give them.

> Almost all critics who have studied the emergence of the literary fairy tale in Europe agree that educated writers purposely appropriated the oral folk tale and converted it into a type of literary discourse about

mores, values, and manners so that children would become civilized according to the social code of that time. The writers of fairy tales for children *acted* ideologically by presenting their notions regarding social conditions and conflicts, and they *interacted* with each other and with past writers and storytellers of folklore in a public sphere.

(Zipes, 1988, p. 3)

Social codes and social attitudes, such as the one we are concerned with here, the accepted social attitude towards stepmothers, are preserved and perpetuated through children's literature and the media.

It is intriguing to examine the changes the story of Cinderella has undergone over time, to note which features of the story have remained constant and which versions have been lost in favour of others. Although the stepmother is a constant, other aspects vary. For example, the Cinderella we know now from a range of books and films and even pantomime versions, is a pleasant girl, clean in spite of her rags, who accepts her lot in life. Our culture values girls who are clean and pleasant and accepting, but in earlier versions of the story Cinderella was a surly and angry girl, rather sluttish and looking for revenge. Cinderella's father is curiously absent but fathers are often involved in the outside world in unseen ways, and our culture accepts that managing the home and children is female business. In earlier periods there was more concern about the role of Cinderella's father. A moral is drawn from his behaviour in Basile's *The Pentamerone* (1634), one of the earliest published collections. As each story is told, the reaction of listeners is described, followed by a parable to explain the meaning of the story. The Cinderella story in this collection is called *The Cat Cinderella* and is based on one of its many variants. (In 1893 Marion Cox published a book with 345 variants of the Cinderella story.) At the close of the tale of *The Cat Cinderella* the listeners were perfectly still and 'passed a verdict of imbecility on the foolish King, [Cinderella's father], who for a silly trifle had exposed the happiness of his own flesh and blood and the succession of the State to such a risk' (p. 56 of the 1848 translation by J. E. Taylor). While the listeners were concerned at the King's neglect of his child and her inheritance and blamed him for Cinderella's sufferings, the storyteller drew attention to a second moral – the stepmother's envy and how it brought about her own downfall.

The stepmother's envy and cruelty and the way they rebound upon herself is a theme which is consistent in almost all versions of the tale. Cinderella is always a disadvantaged child and is always rescued by supernatural aid, but while the means of rescue is the same, the agent varies. Sometimes the child is rescued by a beast, a bird, or a tree, not a figure recognisable as a 'good mother', as in our contemporary version, the plump and lovable little fairy godmother familiar from the Disney film and books. But the cruel stepmother is there, the source of wrongdoing against the helpless Cinderella, and this is the image known to every child and ingrained in every culture.

However, the contemporary Cinderella, portrayed by successive editing to correspond to nineteenth- and twentieth-century ideals of femininity, is not recognisable in the *Pentamerone* story. The Cat Cinderella has not one, but two stepmothers, since she kills her first stepmother by letting the lid of a chest fall on her. She wants to replace her with a governness, who becomes a cruel stepmother in her turn, pushing her own daughters into favour and relegating Cinderella, or Zezolla as she was called in the source material, to menial tasks. She is neglected and demeaned until befriended by a magic agent, in this version, a magic tree. From here on, the story pattern is familiar to us: there are balls where the Cat Cinderella captures the attention of everyone, especially the most eligible and desirable male.

The Cinderella we know is certainly not a girl who would clamp her stepmother in a chest. In our story, all the wickedness resides in the stepmother. There is an interesting historical antecedent to the murder of the stepmother in *The Cat Cinderella* which is cited in the *Pentamerone*. In the sixth century there was a Queen Fredegund, 'a living example of the vilest stepmother ever imagined in the pages of a fairy book' (*ibid.*, p. 62). She ordered an unknown number of murders and tortures, and was jealous of her own daughter, Rigunth. Rigunth was the daughter of a King, while Fredegund had been a palace maid, and it appears that Rigunth continually declared that she should be mistress, probably for this reason. In any case, Fredegund waited for an opportunity to entice the girl, her daughter, to look at jewels in a large chest, and then attempted to force the lid down on her neck, unsuccessfully, because servants intervened and rescued Rigunth. Note that the actual occurrence of murderous behaviour of a mother was converted into the famous stepmother–stepdaughter tale.

Our modern literary versions of the old stories, no longer evolving through oral repetition, present ideals of femininity and masculinity which continue to affirm active participation for men and passive acceptance for women, and they continue to sanction hatred of stepmothers. Even so, they are less harsh and violent than some of the ancient tales. In a version of the Cinderella story from India, the stepmother works her step-daughter to death in the absence of the father. There is no reincarnation of the dead mother to console and help the child. Stith Thompson (1957) identifies tales with stepmothers which contain anything from incest, vengeance, a curse on future life, false accusations, deceptions, ogres and unnatural cruelty to sheer foolishness on the part of the stepmother. There are stories of rewards to and blessing on stepchildren who provide food to an ungrateful stepmother. The stories of incest, from Iceland to Ireland, echo the Phaedra story in Greek mythology, a stepmother in love with her stepson. There is a poignant tale from India about a stepmother bird which feeds thorns to fledglings, and another from India in which the evil stepmother irritates her two stepsons so much that one kills the other. The stepmother-witch in modern stories, jealous and cruel though she is, has a narrower range of cruelty to exercise and is never incestuous.

The issue of incest, of sexual attraction of stepmother to stepson which appears in the Phaedra myth, did not preoccupy the stepmothers I met. However, the story contains themes which do preoccupy most stepmothers. Phaedra's attraction to her stepson, nearer her own age than the father, turns to hatred when she is rejected. She influences the father, Theseus, against the son, Hippolytus, who is killed by his father's curse. Intervention by the goddess Diana (the fairy godmother? the good mother?) restores Hippolytus to life and removes him from the power of his 'deluded father and false stepmother' (Bulfinch, 1947). Here are the themes of confusion and ambiguity which almost always exist in the stepmother–stepchild relationship: incongruous age relationships, powerful feelings of love and rejection turning to hatred, inappropriate sexual attraction – which could be a stepson's towards a young stepmother or a stepfather's towards a stepdaughter – the potential for destructive actions. The stepmothers I talked to admitted having had feelings of hatred towards their stepchildren at times, but not unmitigated hatred; the negative feelings alternate with feelings of affection and protection and wanting to do their best. One stepmother described this as 'evil' feelings mixed with loving ones, both surprising her with their intensity. In biographies I found examples of stepmothers who succeeded in creating satisfying and positive relationships with their stepchildren and in fictional literature there are stories of sympathetic stepmother characters as well as evil ones. However, some of the fictional stepmothers are as unbelievably virtuous as those in folk tales are totally villianous. Flesh and blood women are neither.

Contemporary theories about the mother–child relationship offer some explanation as to why stepmothers appear as they do in myth and legend and folk tradition. I have suggested that the stepmother character was a handy one for the moralists who collected the fairy stories to use in presenting the antithesis to the desired feminine traits they wished to extol. The stepmother was already there in the tradition as a symbol of harshness and absence of affection. How do we explain her prevalence in folk tales from every part of the world? One theory is that because we all have a mother on whom we are totally dependent in early life for food, protection, affection and acceptance, and because our need for her love is so great, to hate her would be unthinkable, nor can we bear to imagine that a mother could be cruel and rejecting, or sexually aroused by her child, though we know this is sometimes the case. The strong, ambivalent feelings we all have towards the mother, who is the source of love but is also terrible in her power, are resolved by separating these feelings and investing them in two figures. Mothers, therefore, become idealised, and cruel mothers become witches and stepmothers. The unthinkable is metaphorically projected onto the stepmother; hatred of mothers and mother figures, thereby, becomes concentrated in the stepmother and can be safely expressed through stories. Historical examples of cruel stepmothers are highlighted by the story telling, the stories in turn appear to be confirmed, and counter-examples are lost.

In Jung's system of archetypes the mother archetype has a

dual nature: on one side she means solicitude and sympathy, with magic authority and all that is benign, cherishing and sustaining. On the other side she connotes secrecy, hidden and devouring powers, and all that is terrifying and inescapable (Jung, 1959, ed. Sir Herbert Read). The tradition of story telling demonstrates this duality. Two stereotypes emerge in twentieth-century versions of fairy stories: the idealised mother and the wicked stepmother.

Iona and Peter Opie (1974) have a different and non-psychological explanation for the frequency with which step-mothers appear in fairy-tales:

> Indeed some details. . .may merely reflect social conditions when the tales were formulated. The prevalence of stepmothers is accounted for by the shortness of life in past times, by the consequent shortness of marriages, and by the practice of the surviving partner marrying again without unnecessary delay. . . .Fairy-tales are thus more realistic than they may appear at first sight; while the magic in them almost heightens the realism. (p. 16)

The Opies make no effort to account for the one-dimensional aspect of the stepmother. They go on to say that there is no general theory to account for why tales appear across cultures and countries and are handed down through many ages; they say the tales may have different meanings in different times and places. We could assume that the presence of a stepmother figure made possible the explication of a particular theme or type of story, and that the significance of the story was thus not stepmothers or neglected children, but greed or poverty, for example. The moral which follows the telling of Cinderella in Perrault's collection (first published in 1698) states that grace is more important than a handsome face, and 'the true, the only, fairies' gift'. Thus it is a tale about the relative values of grace and beauty, and it has a second moral: The gifts of heaven – courage and wit and steadfastness – are greater than the ones that come from earth, and to convert our talents into gain we need to possess godmothers, or godfathers. The hapless stepmother and her awful behaviour provide the background against which to present the moral lesson. She represents the evil and wrongdoing in the world which have to be overcome by heavenly aid. Unfortunately, every stepmother has to contend with being labelled as an evil force.

Cinderella has had a stepmother in all known versions of the story but one. The final version in Cox's book, the three hundred and forty-fifth, is an ancient variant, translated from Gaelic, in which a child is aided by magic because of jealousy, but there is no abuse, and no stepmother (Cox, 1893). But as we have seen, Cinderella has not always been a child 'of unparalleled goodness' with a 'sweetness of temper' inherited from her mother, 'who was the best creature in the world' (Perrault, 1729, p. 73). (Has any stepmother not felt she was being compared to a perfect mother?) Cinderella has become the symbol of female purity and gentleness as the stepmother has become the symbol of the opposite. Peter Laslett refers to the Cinderella tale as 'that influential piece of mischievous make-believe' (Laslett, 1977, p. 172). Mischievous seems too mild a word to describe the influence of the oldest (the earliest datable version occurs in a Chinese book written about AD 850–60), best-known and best-loved fairy story in the world which provides an important piece of the context in which contemporary stepmothers attempt to fulfil their role. There is nothing in a woman's experience or cultural inheritance which gives her confidence or tells her she will gain approval as a stepmother, and much which tells her she will not.

We know that stepmothers have been substituted for other characters in some stories, as, for example, in *Hansel and Gretel*. Not until the Grimm Brothers published their collection in 1812 did Hansel and Gretel have a stepmother. In the earlier versions, upon which the Grimms drew, the story was about impover-ished parents who abandoned their children because they could not feed them (Opie and Opie, 1974). Similarly, *The Story of Snow White and the Seven Dwarfs* – a story which, the Opies say, is not necessarily ancient and varies little over a wide area from Ireland to Asia Minor and North and West Africa – more commonly features jealousy as a general theme rather than hatred of a step-child. As the story is told in the *Pentamerone*, the queen is Snow White's aunt. In the Grimm Brothers' collection, however, the queen is her stepmother, and it is this version which Walt Disney used in 1938 to make his famous film. It is significant that during the period that stepmother figures were being utilised as the universal symbol of cruelty to children in the collections of fairy stories, the process of idealising motherhood and women as mothers was simultaneously taking place (Dally, 1982). In this way the stories children absorb become part of social attitudes supported in other areas of cultural life.

That the power of the cultural image of stepmothers through fairy stories has not waned is demonstrated by this excerpt from the newsletter of the National Stepfamily Association (No. 12, Summer 1986):

> I have often felt that stepmothers – like mothers-in-law – just can't win. Jokes, plays, films, stories old and new, all show us up in the worst possible light. . . .the following story illustrates my point. Louise, my stepdaughter, was trying to answer the questions Luke, her five-year-old son, was asking about why she had had two mothers. Naturally in her explanations she used the term stepmother to refer to me. Luke became indignant, began to protest and eventually cried. 'I love grandma, she's nice, she isn't a stepmother' was the gist of his protests. Louise was mystified until she realised that Luke had recently been told *The Story of Snow White* at school. . . . I was deeply touched to think that Luke refused to accept me as the wicked stepmother but, as I said earlier, almost everyone seems to see us that way. What can we do about it?

In plays and novels the stepmother is presented as a more acceptable human being than in the fairy tales, although in some novels the stepmother becomes the opposite stereotype, the virtuous and selfless female. She appears to change places with Cinderella, doing the work without complaint. An example can be found in a novel, *The Stepmother* (Hutchinson, 1955), in which a woman marries the man to whom she had been secretary and acquires an adult stepson. His idealised mother is dead, disabled early in her adult life and much revered for her courage. Both father and son are frozen in grief, but also harbour unrecognised anger at the influence the dead woman exerts over them. The stepmother nurses her stepson back to health, physical and mental, which involves sensitively making him confront the painful fact that he was idolising his mother, and in the end frees both him and his father from a paralysis of guilt and grief, much of which is anger at the dead woman's stranglehold. The stepmother is both selfless and self-sufficient; she has no supernatural agents, not even a close friend, to help her. This combination of selflessness and self-sufficiency is one which might make for success in stepmothering, but most mortal women would find it almost impossible to attain or sustain.

As we have seen, there is another myth which dogs the life of the stepmother and that is the myth of the perfect mother. Hutchinson's fictional stepmother is the perfect wife/mother/ stepmother and must be understood as a writer's dream, not a writer's interpretation of real life. Hutchinson observes the situation a replacement wife and replacement mother might be in, and then invents a model to solve the problems which fits the cultural ideals for women. He even provides the stepmother with enough money to contemplate leaving her husband and living independently, and to be fair, the stepmother does suffer, does feel depleted and lonely. However, she has made such a good job of healing both her husband and stepson that the possibility of a more fulfilling life makes her stay, and she even has to deal with her stepson's infatuation for her – no Phaedra she – and does this with grace and respect. Where does all her strength come from? We are never told. Real women, on the other hand, have conflicts which defeat them unless there are sufficient supports in their lives.

In 1899 Mrs Alexander published her novel *The Step-Mother*, the story of another woman of unblemished virtue. Here the stepmother cares for her stepchild against the wishes of her husband, who coldly rejects his son. She says to him: ' "I should cherish it, or any forsaken, helpless creature besides", stretching out her hand with an inexpressibly gracious gesture. "Don't you think I should love a child of yours whoever was the mother?" ' He is unmoved, describes her impulse as sickly sentimentality, and tells her he prefers his wife to be guided by him in conduct and opinions. In her rejoinder the theme of the novel is made clear: ' "I am quite willing to be guided by you. . . . but I will never give up my right to form my own opinion, or sink from an individual to an echo." ' Another character in the novel comments upon the wife's right to her own views: ' "she should not renounce her right of judgment at the bidding of any one, even a husband. The day was gone by when blind obedience was part of wifely duty." ' As in the ancient stories, the stepmother is used to highlight other themes, values and morals. Mrs Alexander uses the stepmother to challenge male authority and also the cruel stepmother myth. It is possible that she assumed there would be greater support for and identification with a woman who defied a husband on behalf of a stepchild than on some other issue, but that can only be conjecture.

These two 'good' fictional stepmothers have a number of things in common: both show great strength of mind and purpose, and high moral courage; both are economically independent; neither seems to need affection from her partner, nor suffers from destructive criticism from outsiders and each meets little resistance from her stepchild. Stepmothers looking for guidance and inspiration from these two models will be discouraged by their own lack of such advantages. Again and again the stepmothers to whom I spoke described their sense of isolation, their self-doubt in the face of the child's resistance and efforts to assert primacy with the father, and their need for the support and affection of their partner in their job as stepmother. If a stepmother is experiencing stress coping with her step-children and as a result of her feelings towards them, the irony is, she will find great difficulty in describing the stress or sharing it with her partner. If she does try, she may find he cannot acknowledge it and support her, for he may feel that to do so would be tantamount to taking sides with her against his child. It is common to hear a stepmother say her partner tells her that the children are her problem and her concern, that he has no problems with them. Or she may declare that she cannot talk to him at all about her tension and confusion without an argument developing. It is his understanding she needs and is least likely to have, certainly in the beginning. If such a situation continues chronic misunderstanding will set in between the partners, leading, perhaps, to a separation neither really wanted. Here is a stepmother whose experience is an example:

> 'There's a lot of guilt. You cannot do what you would normally do with your own child, so you feel guilty, but if you do have a normal reaction and get angry, you feel guilty about that, too. You are always so afraid you will be unfair. Her [stepdaughter's] father and I did not agree and he would say I nagged if I disciplined her. The more he did nothing to structure her, the more I seemed to nag. Sometimes I would say to him, "You see me as a person I am not." I wanted to provide something for her, to be an element of the life which was missing, but perhaps I am not flexible enough.'

Flexibility is certainly a quality every stepmother needs, but each will have her own limits. The stepmother above went on to describe how she had been the person caring for her stepdaughter most of the time, day to day, but when decisions were made about the child's life, education, etc., the opinion of the stepmother was disregarded. Eventually the conflict eroded the attraction and understanding between the couple and they parted, but as she reflected on her experience, this woman commented on two issues. One concerned the importance of support from others, loved and important people, which she had lacked in her stepmothering; the other was that it took time for the steprelationship to be valued. Even after several years, and in spite of the divorce from her husband, there was continuing contact between this woman and her stepdaughter; she had succeeded in her goal of providing a needed element in that young person's life.

Real-life experience, recorded in biographies and auto-biographies, attests to the significance of time in enhancing steprelationships. The life of Abraham Lincoln provides an example. He had a stepmother who was a capable and determined woman. She raised a large family of children and stepchildren and her life was one of hard work, but she also took an interest in education which previously no one had done in Lincoln's family. Although she herself could not read, she encouraged the children to learn and found that her stepson was an avid reader. She said of Abraham Lincoln as a boy, 'His mind and mine, what little I had, seemed to run together, move in the same channel' (Lorant, 1954, p. 13). Biographers tell us that Lincoln and his stepmother shared a sense of humour, surely a vital ingredient in a lasting relationship. The story of Lincoln's wife, Mary Todd Lincoln, and her stepmother is the antithesis, however. It was an unhappy relationship and time did not improve it.

In fact, I was frustrated in my efforts to locate stepmothers in biographical material; they tend not be be featured. One that was featured, because she wrote about her stepdaughter, was Lady Florence Bell. Gertrude Bell was a remarkable woman, a traveller and diplomatist, Arabic scholar, gardener and naturalist. When she died in 1926 her letters were collected and published by her stepmother. Lady Bell wrote with sensitive appreciation of the closeness between Gertrude Bell and her father, celebrating their 'companionship and deep mutal affection. . .to both the very foundation of existence until the day she died' (Bell, 1927, p. 5). In being able to honour and mourn her stepdaughter and not, apparently, feel excluded by the closeness between her husband and his daughter, Lady Bell demonstrates a remarkable vision and generosity of spirit. She found a way of being a stepmother which functioned well in her situation. There must have been many contributing factors that helped her to do this, one of the most significant of which was surely that she and Gertrude Bell knew each other before they became step-relations. It is more usual for stepmothers to have little prior acquaintance with the children, or young adults, to whom they become stepmother.

Biographies that record positive relationships between stepmothers and their stepchildren provide a small but welcome antidote to the fairy tales and their unremittingly negative images. And biographical evidence from ordinary people – material that is seldom written down or published – provides much additional support. Very few children welcome a stepmother in the first instance; their insecurities are too great at the point at which a stepmother enters their lives. As adults, however, their retrospective view is at least as often positive as negative. In an analysis of twenty-eight life-story interviews with men and women born between 1880 and 1904, who had grown up in stepfamilies, Burchardt (1987) found a mixture of good and bad memories, with memories of stepmothers consistently provoking stronger emotion than those of stepfathers. Again, the fact that fathers are more distant from family life than mothers and, therefore, have a different set of expectations to fulfil, explains the difference in the intensity of memories of stepfathers. However, an equal number of stepmothers were remembered positively as negatively.

A stepchild, a young person describing her stepmother, recently wrote:

> The stereotype of the wicked stepmother must have some basis in fact; yet my own experience as a stepchild shows that it is possible to have a friendly relationship. . . .We established an amicable relationship. . .though I did not regard W. . .as a mother, and I would have resented it if she had expected me to. . . .Our relationship isn't as close as that between natural parents and their children but there are certain benefits in this. Stepparents can be more detached, and there's no danger of them seeing the child as an extension of themselves.

Sometimes, because they're less involved, it is easier for them to see where the child's real interests lie.

(National Stepfamily Association Newsletter, Spring, 1987)

Not only does this young person regard her stepmother positively, she seems to be able to do this while keeping her loyalty to her natural mother intact. She has not made a split between a good mother and a bad stepmother, possibly because, as she says, her stepmother did not attempt to replace, or displace, her own mother. In contrast to this account, however, is a letter from a fifteen-year-old written to the Stepfamily Association:

> I can't stand my stepmother. . .she really is wicked. She always orders me around, and if I cheek her, she pretends to get upset and runs to my dad, then he and I have an argument. . . .To make it worse, I can't tell my mum, she'd probably kill [my stepmother].

The writer is angry with all three of the adults, but it is the 'wicked' stepmother who is the main target of her anger.

We cannot look to plays, novels or stories, for answers or directives; these are found in the process of living and exploring the resources in one's life situation. But literature, together with works on sociology and psychology, can illuminate our own experience. By examining the cultural images which shape our lives, we can widen our outlook, challenge accepted attitudes, make choices, and at the very least, recognise commonalities in human experience. Every stepmother I interviewed, without exception, described a sense of personal failure and isolation which either had been severe, or was severe at the time of the interview. And in the plays or novels I have read, the stepmother, whether a paragon of virtue or unpleasant and destructive, whether powerful or feeble, would be allowed by the author to show bewilderment and a sense of failure, giving the work of creation a validity confirmed by the stepmothers I met. This held true for obscure works written centuries ago and for contemporary literature.

As an example: in the mid seventeenth century Sir Robert Stapleton wrote a play, *The Step-Mother: A Tragi-Comedy*, 'Acted with great applause at the Theatre in Little Lincolns-Inn-Fields by His Highness the Duke of York's Servants' (title page of the 1664 edition). It is set in post-Roman Britain; the protaganists are, of course, persons of power. The stepmother is a princess by both her marriages, but the terms of her power and wealth are unclear. As a widow, however, her ownership of property and title to wealth would be secure, and so she plots the death of her second husband. She is an object of suspicion in many quarters – her stepchildren, also her own children towards whom she has become a changed person. They discuss her: 'My Mother used to give us better Precepts. . . .She was good-natur'd, and had a sense of Honour. . .And of Religion; but now she leaves/The Temples of the Gods, to consult Witches.' The stepmother, Portia, has no friend, even her religious beliefs fail her, and her son and stepson become sworn friends and side against her. There is a resolution however, and when Portia achieves it, that is, establishes her rights and resources, she asks her husband, children and stepchildren, for forgiveness. In an epilogue she asks the audience to judge her; she asks them to consider what they would have done in her place.

Similarly, Frederick Howard, 5th Earl of Carlisle, author of a play written over a hundred years later, understands the ambiguity of a stepmother's role and its effects on her behaviour and closest relationships. The stepmother brings wealth to her second marriage and then discovers that she is excluded from her second husband's will and her stepson inherits all. In this play, *Step-Mother* (Howard, 1800), the stepmother is hated and feared – 'There she goes,/To make e'en charity itself disgusting . . . .Our conference will excite her jealousy,/And we shall feel her vengeance' – but we are made to understand that she is reacting to being caught in a situation which has rendered her powerless and isolated. She says: 'to rob me from the grave . . .when his shrouded eyes no more could feast/With execrable joy on the oppression,/Still to oppress – O this dissolves all ties!' By becoming a stepmother, not only has she lost what she possessed in real terms, but she has lost affection and self-respect. Surely the author intends us to understand that she is doubly disinherited.

Disputes over property and inheritance are not uncommon in contemporary stepfamily life, either. Not long ago, a woman asked for help with a stepfamily problem and came to see me. Her husband, she felt, could not resolve his guilt over the ending of his first marriage, to the extent that he wished to make his children by his first marriage the heirs to the home his second wife owned before they met. She also had children. The couple could not agree how their resources should be allocated. As they struggled to resolve the disagreements, affection and trust were disappearing, a loss she felt keenly. She wanted another child but he was reluctant to commit himself because it would be only a further drain on him emotionally and financially. It seemed to her that the only way to have his affection was to buy it by agreeing to come second in every way.

Novels provide abundant scope for exploring the complexities in family relationships. In *Wives and Daughters* (1866), Mrs Gaskell depicts one of the dilemmas of the stepmother, that of the outsider. In this story the stepmother is not deliberately cruel, but she is self-centred and shallow and is cruel because she lacks perception. Although she is not wise, she realises that she is an outsider to the close and loving understanding that exists between her husband and his daughter. She cannot reach either of them and in the end is merely tolerated. Mrs Gaskell also lets us see the devastation of the child when a parent takes a new partner. When the child, Molly, learns of her father's intention to marry, 'It was as if the piece of solid ground on which she stood had broken from the shore, and she was drifting out to the infinite sea alone.' She accepts the inevitable, but feels that her father has ceased not only to love her, but has forgotten her dead mother, and later she puts her finger on another common issue in stepfamilies when she tells another character, 'You know we didn't know much of each other before we were put to live together.' The conflict of loyalties, the child's sense of abandonment, the lack of preparation before the stepmother appeared on the scene and the particularly difficult combination of stepmother and adolescent stepdaughter competing to look after the husband and father are all well observed and explored. There is an echo of Cinderella in the character of Molly, who is very, very good and lovable. 'If Molly had not had the sweetest disposition in the world she might have become jealous [of her stepsister]. . .but she never thought of comparing the amount of admiration and love which they each received.'

Very, very few stepmothers set out with evil intentions towards their stepchildren. Mrs Gaskell's story is of a weak and inadequate woman, not a malicious one. She tries to do the right

thing, to be a good substitute mother as far as she is able. Most
stepmothers set out with ideals about putting things right in
their stepchildren's lives, and become disillusioned when their
efforts seem to fail or the children reject them. The stepmother,
culturally conditioned as all women are to be a mother, will take
on stepchildren she may hardly know, and assume all the
nurturing, feeding, disciplining, as if she had known them from
birth. The children resist and the stepmother is baffled, and feels
she is an outsider whose good intentions are misunderstood. In
another nineteenth-century novel, Charlotte M. Yonge draws a
portrait of a young woman who sets to work, in spite of her
family's opposition, to bring new life to three grieving
stepchildren and their father, and fill the place of a lost mother
(*The Young Stepmother; Or a chronicle of mistakes*, 1861). She
becomes weary and discouraged:

> [She] had a sad, sore sense of failure, and almost of guilt, as she
> lingered on the doorstep. . . .the education of 'Edmund's children' had
> been a cherished vision, and it had resulted so differently from her
> expectations, that her heart sank. . . . 'You know I meant to do my
> best, but they were right, I was too young. . . . What visions I had
> about those three, and what failures have resulted!'

Her mistake actually is to assume that she can create love and
trust instantly; she criticises and cajoles the children and
challenges family history and ways of doing things when she
herself is the newcomer and, in the children's eyes, an
interloper. Eventually she does succeed in creating love and
trust, but never ceases to feel that whatever her stepchildren
suffer in their lives is her fault and the result of her failing. This
again is a cultural message to women as mothers, and it is
addressed to stepmothers as well; it says that whatever befalls
children is the mother's responsibility. It is echoed in the words
of this stepmother:

> **'They are grown up now, and living their own adult lives. But
> whenever they have a trouble in their lives we ask ourselves if it
> is because of our family situation, because they were step-
> children, and I wasn't good enough.'**

Some stepmothers are not good enough, and some fail
bitterly. When the memories of a stepmother are bitter, they are
bitter indeed. Robert Liddell wrote an autobiographical novel
about his own stepmother which amounts almost to a tirade

against her, a prolonged rage at the sufferings he and his brother experienced (*Stepsons*, 1959). He described it himself as a 'story of family tyranny' (Liddell, 1986, p. 83). That Robert Liddell's childhood was oppressive there can be no doubt, but in his attack on his father's second wife he puts the entire blame for his unhappiness on her. He does not criticise his father for his passivity, for his increasing lack of involvement in his children's lives; he prefers to see him as a victim also. The two little boys, still grieving for their mother, are living with indulgent aunts when their lives are again in turmoil with their father's remarriage. The story, fictional but based on actual life experience, highlights many of the most painful issues that stepmothers and stepchildren have to face. The children are unprepared for her entry into their lives and, at the same time, are aware of their aunts' disapproval of their father's decision. The presence of a stepmother makes the finality of the loss of a mother, or the ending of the parents' marriage, inescapable. In this book the reality of their mother's death is borne in upon the children:

> Moreover, the advent of a stepmother made his mother's death an established fact. . . . Andrew knew that all stepmothers were wicked, and reasoned that a German stepmother was likely to be more wicked than most. The aunts said as little as possible, but their disapproval was patent.
>
> (Liddell, 1959)

Against this background of prejudice, lack of preparation, resentment and sorrow, the stepmother enters their lives and tries to be 'mother'. Her wish to have children herself is not shared by her husband, and she envies him and her dead predecessor the intimacy of children:

> She could see that Oswald had no great wish to have a second family, and would be more than content for her to be a mother to the first. . . . She tried not to face this thought; it was not for the sake of another woman's children that she had gone through her training. It was at this time that she began to conceive a jealous hatred against Frances and the two little boys. (*ibid.*)

The stepmother's life is tormented, but her behaviour, while understandable, is unforgivable. She takes to committing acts of petty cruelty which make the children feel unwelcome in their own home. They hate her and feel hated by her. 'Andrew

prayed fiercely and urgently in his bath, with the faith that dares
to ask for and to expect miracles: "O God, who in Thy wrath
gavest us a stepmother, in Thy mercy remove her." ' A cycle of
attack and withdrawal is established. The stepmother's presence
is compared to a family curse with echoes of the lowering hatred
of Greek tragedy; she becomes more and more isolated. The
children have each other,

> [They] amused and comforted themselves with a fantasy about the
> Society for the Prevention of Stepmothers; it might be a sub-branch of
> the Society for Prevention of Cruelty to Children. . .[an] Inspector
> might make surprise visits now and then, to hear the stepchildren's
> complaints, or to see for himself. . . .She was now every inch a
> stepmother; there was no other relationship in life for which she was
> qualified.

Ivy Compton-Burnett, who wrote about families – and
mostly unhappy ones – in all her novels, was a friend of
Liddell's; she admired *Stepsons*, but confessed that she 'could not
help feeling a pang of sympathy for that awful woman' (Francis
King, introduction to Liddell, 1986). In turn Liddell noted that
Ivy Compton-Burnett

> In all the family relations she has explored. . .has not given us a
> wicked stepmother. . .who upsets everything by her entry into the
> family: her Unhappy Families are already set, and her sympathies are
> on the side of the newcomers who always have difficulty in entering
> the already crowded scene.
>
> (Liddell, 1955, p. 79)

Ivy Compton-Burnett's own family was a crowded scene. Her
father had a first family of five children and a second family of
seven, of whom Ivy was the eldest. This large combination of
half-siblings to whom Ivy's mother was both mother and
stepmother, a 'double family' as she called it, was not happy.
The eldest daughter of the first family had become a close
companion to her father after her mother's death and was
bitterly jealous of her stepmother. And in fact, the second Mrs
Compton-Burnett was not tactful with her stepchildren; she
treated them as members of a different and lesser family, 'and in
consequence remained for them an intruder' (Sprigge, 1973,
p. 23). She was, apparently, a rather distant and tyrannical
mother, even to her own children. Her eldest stepdaughter
always called her 'Mrs Burnett' and in her turn, remained aloof

from the second family. This stepdaughter was the eldest child of the first marriage, while Ivy Compton-Burnett was the eldest of the second, but when both the parents were dead, under the terms of her mother's will, Ivy became head of the family and grew into something of a tyrant herself. However, she and her brothers and sisters adjusted the family finances to help their half-siblings who had been disadvantaged by the provisions of their father's will. He died first, left everything to his wife, trusting her to be fair to the children of his first marriage in her own will; unfortunately she was not.

Compton-Burnett lived in a complex and unhappy family situation; some members were distant and estranged, others, in pairs, were desperately close, compensating for the tension and conflicts around them. Two of her sisters committed suicide together; she was very close to a brother who was killed during World War I. As a novelist, she observed the complex relationships and the suffering and reproduced much of it; the themes of power and the tyrannical use of it appear in all her books, but she also saw that the tyrant is a victim too: In *Parents and Children*, written in 1955, one of the characters says,

> 'Of course stepmothers are cruel. . .but then so are stepchildren, though they don't have any of the discredit. We all have a right to survive, and only the fittest can so do, and it seems that a struggle is inevitable.'

It is possible to argue that these examples from fiction are obscure or irrelevant; Sir Robert Stapleton and Sir Frederick Howard are hardly popular reading; even Compton-Burnett is an acquired taste. But to argue on those lines would be to miss the point. Throughout literature, from *The Story of Cinderella* to the most obscure play or novel, the stepmother nearly always appears as a problematic and ambiguous character, at the very least. Every stepmother suffers as a result. Cultural images reflect society's attitudes and determine, to a greater or lesser extent, a stepmother's lot. As this latter-day stepmother put it:

> **'Society's attitude to stepmothers is unrealistic. On the one hand there is only one adjective which springs to mind and that is "wicked". On the other hand, stepmothers are expected to behave as if they were biological mothers. Such an unrealistic expectation and subsequent failure to meet it fuels the myth of being wicked. Whilst, clearly, most women know when they**

marry a man that he has children – although this is not always so – and the children should be a part of the decision making as to whether she will or will not marry the man, the children are consequences of that decision rather than chosen in their right – as are children who are adopted or fostered or planned to be born. Thus, the woman has no choice in accepting them, but has considerable obligations placed on her. These obligations frequently seem to exceed those which were anticipated by her. Furthermore, society seems to have found a neat solution to its problems by preferring to assume that the stepmother should be the same as a mother. A stepmother's position is however extremely ambiguous, for example in the law, and this probably more nearly reflects society's own ambiguous attitudes.'

CHAPTER THREE

A woman, a stepmother

Women are trained to be mothers from babyhood, we grow up with that, so give us a little kid and we start to feel we ought to mother it, and we might not want to mother it. And once you start to mother you have to be the good mother and never disappoint or make the child unhappy.

A stepmother

. . .but presently she perceived that innumerable little strands like the thread of a spider were fastening themselves round her wrists and ankles, and that each one of them ran up to its other end in somebody's heart. . . .and as for her mother's heart, that might have been a railway terminus, so many shining threads ran up into it out of sight – threads of pride and love and relief and maternal agitation and feminine welcome of fuss.

All Passion Spent, Vita Sackville-West

Has any woman ever aspired to be a stepmother? Although many women do aspire to have children, and all women know they are supposed to wish for them, no woman dreams of becoming a stepmother. It just happens, an accident, in the course of living, and loving a man who is already a father. Though a stranger to the intense intimacy of their early family life, she assumes an ancient and common role for women, one that everyone knows about. The deeply-ingrained knowledge that children may suffer at the hands of a stepmother, and do always suffer when they lose their mother, is enough to make many women take on stepmotherhood with the selfless determination to make their life happy, to defy the cruel stepmother myth and to fulfil the 'mother role' in every possible way, except biologically. An adoptive mother does not need biology to enable her to meet the needs of her children. Why should a stepmother? It is true that, unlike an adoptive mother, she does not elect to take on her role, nor does she choose her stepchildren and she is unlikely to have known them from babyhood. In a sense, being a successful stepmother is the ultimate achievement in mothering, because it involves coping with just about all of the disadvantages and difficulties of being a mother but having few of the advantages. It is an achievement in mothering beyond even fostering deprived or handicapped children. A woman who fosters children knows her maternal capacities, having tried and tested them through experience, she knows she has the admiration and support of society, and she receives payment for the job she does. A stepmother, on the other hand, does not have society's approval for the job she does, and she has no contract for it except with the father of the children. It seems she cannot fail in her stepmothering without failing to some degree in her relationship with him. If she succeeds, she succeeds richly indeed.

Because a woman bears the children and traditionally undertakes most of the nurturing in the early years, when she becomes a stepmother she will imagine she must take on a maternal role in relation to her partner's children. She is a woman, they are children, therefore, she must 'mother' them. When she experiences their rejection of her efforts to mother them – for example, when they do not eat what she has cooked, or when they ask their father for permission to do simple things, or when they ask their father to confirm her directions to them, or in many other ways show they do not accept her as having a parental relationship to them – the stepmother experiences a sense of betrayal. She feels betrayed by her own feelings, which she realises are not 'right', and betrayed by the children who, she feels, do not recognise or accept her 'mothering'. Her sense of confusion and helplessness, coupled with the shock that she does not feel the affection and love for the children she wants and expects to feel, may cause her deep shame. Usually, she tries harder, the children harden their resistence, and both parties become trapped in a vicious circle.

Every girl grows up with a powerful destiny – to become a mother in her time. Little girls play at being mother and rehearse the role again and again in the richness of childhood fantasy, endlessly varying the scenarios. They occasionally play at being sisters, aunts or grandmothers, or even pets and, of course, princesses are favourites for weaving into domestic play. Witches may appear and so may Wonderwoman and Supergirl, but the popularity of mother and baby never wanes. Millions of little girls tuck millions of dolls into make-believe beds in make-believe homes. They instruct one another in child-care and role management in endless scenarios of family life, and fend off the attack of monsters or Superman, which most little boys prefer to domestic play – or do after the age of 4 or 5. Three-year-old boys indulge in domestic play in a similar way to girls, exchanging male and female roles without concern. 'Mother, father and baby are the primary actors, but identities shift and participants seldom keep one another informed' (Paley, 1984, p. x). Boys offer to be mother or father, whichever is needed, and a girl may dress up in male outfits and cuddle the baby. But after the age of 5 or 6, both boys and girls are resolving lingering doubts or confusion about gender identity – 'I am a boy', 'I am a girl' – through fantasy play which segregates gender behaviour – 'If I am a boy, I do this'; 'If I am girl, I do this.' Play is serious business for children, as teachers and students of child development know, and 'a major vehicle for socialisation' (Monighan-Nourot, et al., 1987).

Fantasy play is the 'stronghold against ambiguity' (Paley, 1984, p. ix), the arena for exploring gender and social roles, and for exercising the imagination. It is the safe place to play out fears and confusion about roles as well as difficult or painful experiences; play is the most effective tension reliever available to children. Yet, I doubt that little girls play at being stepmothers in the range of female roles they utilise. The mother role enjoys unconditional social approval; society's attitude to the stepmother is too negative. Where can little girls find social rules for making the stepmother the good mother, the all-protective, all-love, mother?

Paley spent a year recording the play of the five-year-old children in her classroom and transcribing it, and I can find no mention of a stepmother. Perhaps stepmothers were represented by the witch parts or appeared only when the fairy tales were being acted out, disguised, because I never found the step-mother figure mentioned by name. The children certainly knew the traditional tales, and liked them read in their traditional form, but when they were acted out, or used in fantasy play, they were heavily altered by the children. Stepmothers were 'edited out', everyone was well protected by magic, or magical strength. Girls seemed to use magic to ensure that the characters were cared for, while boys used strength, a different form of power. The children analysed and chose the characters to invent their stories and scenarios. The following is a version in which the emphasis is on the romance between Snow White and the prince: 'Once upon a time there was a girl named Snow White and there was a prince and he loved that girl. And he always loved her like a rose. He loved her so so so much better than the time before. And one day they met each other at the pond and they saw seven dwarfs' (Paley, p. 9). No wicked queen or stepmother ever appeared. What 'the time before' refers to we do not know. The speaker is a girl, of course. The girls used the Cinderella character often, and mixed it with whatever was the current theme, which was never stepmothers. Mothers figure in and are added, when necessary, to stories invented by both boys and girls. Here a little girl puts several fairy stories together, creates a crisis, and takes care of the characters as well:

> 'I'm Cinderella', Charlotte decides. 'You be Snow White.' She and Mary Ann will be sisters who live in a brick house with no chimney, in a wood that has no wolf. 'Pretend our mother is poor and we got lost and then we see a brick house that's empty.' 'But really a godmother lives there —' 'And she's taking a walk and then she sees the two little girls and she's not angry.' (*ibid.*, p. 47)

Although the children in Paley's class – and I feel safe in generalising from their behaviour – made changes in all the fairy stories, as already stated, they wanted the familiar, traditional version to be read to them, and they discussed it before making their changes. For example, both the boys and the girls were concerned about Goldilocks; she has no family, no skills and no magic to assist her. The children in Paley's class thought of ways to help: they invented a picnic and invited Cinderella, but Goldilocks had to go home by herself. They decided she was a housebreaker and robber, and then a homeless orphan, but they never wanted to 'be' her in their play like the girls who took on the roles of Cinderella or Snow White. Those two famous females have magical aid and end up with a prince, while Goldilocks has no visible supports of any kind. The girls were either ordinary household females without threat from wolves or witches, or they were princesses with magic to aid them in distress. In their play, however dangerous the situation, there was a mother or fairy godmother to put things right. What they were doing had tremendous significance for them. They were rationalising their gender identity – 'I am a girl because I am doing this' – and through play were discovering the meaning of being a girl (or boy). Girls are mothers, or princesses, and the magic that rescues them comes from a female, the fairy godmother. Boys play games in which a show of strength deals with difficulties; this is the way the 'good guy' overcomes the 'bad guy'. The boys' games are noisy and full of conflict as they decide who is good or bad. The play of the girls, although noisy at times, moves towards a lessening of tension and a resolution of conflict, even if supernatural aid is required to attain it. Girls learn early that their job is to be tension regulators, mothers with magic. We should note, however, that even after the age of 5 or 6 more scope is allowed girls in their play than boys.

> Except for commercial celebrities such as Princess Leia and Wonder-woman, boys scrupulously disregard female characters. . . .[a girl] can play in any fashion without embarrassment. A boy in a frilly bedjacket expects to be laughed at, but a superhero cape on a girl creates no stir. There is nothing illusory about female adaptability – or male intransigence – in matters of fantasy play. (*ibid.*, p. 102)

If little girls do not incorporate stepmothers into fantasy play, it may be because the stepmother is the opposite pole from the favourite figure, the fairy godmother. Or it may be because of what is implied by having a stepmother. In fantasy play mothers get lost but are found again or restored by magic. Whatever the reasons, many, many women find themselves playing a role which they have never rehearsed, and which has only one model, a model which is totally unsuitable.

The model for being a mother which women in the West draw upon is based upon an idealisation which has these features: selflessness, self-sacrifice, and self-reliance. The good mother is wise, strong, reliable and durable; she puts the child's needs before her own. Her love for the child is continuous and unwavering; she is always present, always available to the child. She teaches, nurtures, comforts and controls unstintingly, and assumes total responsibility for the child, especially in its early years. She spends most of her time alone with the child and is always responsive. Whatever her personal interests, ambitions

or training, she will forego participation in public affairs while
the child is growing up, and she knows that whatever goes
wrong in the life of a child is the result of 'bad' mothering. The
good mother is never ambivalent about being a mother; she
rejoices in her children and her concern for them is passionate
and limitless. Society expects all this of a woman simply because
she is a woman; it assumes that she is born with an instinct for
mothering. Thus, it becomes accepted that only a woman
contains the virtues needed to be mother, that only after she has
given birth has a woman fulfilled her destiny and, furthermore,
that only a woman who has given birth can love a child with
true maternal self-denial.

Some women have these gifts, some do not. Some men have
these gifts also, just as there are women who can 'mother'
without giving birth. Both the ideal and the assumptions may
be challenged, but before exploring the challenges, consider
how stepmothers might be affected by the ideal of mother love
and care. The two basic requirements built into the role of
mother are full-time care of children and sole responsibility for
them (Barnard, 1975). These two structure the way the job of
being a mother is carried out. The mother cares for children; if
she works outside the home, her work takes second place and
she must make arrangements for child-care to cover her
absence. Such arrangements must be satisfactory, and if they are
not, it is the mother who must make changes, either in her
work, or in the child-care.

For a full-time, or custodial, stepmother who has not had
children of her own, there is no gradual transition to the total
commitment required in the mother role. If she has children
herself, she knows what is involved, but still may not be
prepared for the sudden thrust into caring emotionally, physically and psychologically for children who may be strangers to
her, and to whom she is a stranger. She knows too that the
social expectation is that she will be at home caring for the
children herself. A part-time, or non-custodial, stepmother,
whose children do not live with her but see her only when they
have contact with their father, has a slightly easier time in that
she has less responsibility, but the expectation that she will care
for the children as if they were her own still prevails. Both
custodial and non-custodial stepmothers will find themselves in
emotional competition with the children's mother.

The conflict between the ideal of the selfless mother and the image of the unloving stepmother can trap a stepmother in a worsening spiral which has this sort of pattern: she expects to love and 'mother' her stepchildren and it is expected of her. She, society and her partner, expect an attachment between her and her stepchildren to form instantaneously. When these unrealistic expectations are not fulfilled, the stepmother feels guilty and inadequate. She then begins to resent the stepchildren for exposing her inability to live up to social and emotional expectations. She feels isolated, her resentment increases and she may actually treat the stepchildren unfairly. Her guilt feelings increase as a result and, in an attempt to relieve them, she begins to think the stepchildren are simply unlovable, or else she decides that she herself is totally to blame. She suffers low self-esteem. Stress between her and her partner sets in because her partner feels torn between his children and her. What is more, he considers that mothering is her concern, not his. He cannot support her in the stress she is experiencing because he simply cannot understand it. She probably criticises him for indulging or not controlling his children adequately, and this puts him on the defensive.

If the stepmother seeks outside help, there is a strong chance she will receive the same cultural message she started out with – that she must love and mother her stepchildren. Many step-mothers described such experiences and several recounted the reactions of their own mothers:

> **'When I tried to talk to my mother she just told me to get on with it, that I knew what I was getting into. But I didn't know, and no one does. I didn't know how much generosity it takes to be a stepmother, and I certainly didn't know about the awful feelings of jealousy toward a child! How do you begin to love a child when all that is happening?'**

The cycle may go on repeating itself for years, until the children grow up and move away, or until the couple's relationship disintegrates, or until the partners find a way to understand each other's experience and offer mutual support, or perhaps until there is contact with someone with similar experience or special knowledge, who can help to restore the stepmother's self-esteem by telling her that her responses are not deviant, but are common and even universal.

There is general agreement amongst researchers and clinicians that the stepmother role is more difficult and demanding than the stepfather one (Fast and Cain, 1966; Duberman, 1975) and continues to be the most misunderstood role in the stepfamily constellation (Morrison and Thompson-Guppy, 1985). Some state that the most intense levels of stepfamily stress flow from the position of the stepmother (John and Emily Visher, personal communication, 1987; Elizabeth Carter, address to conference: 'Couples in Crisis', Rome, 1987). In the traditional gender roles women take the responsibility for the emotional life of the family and are the tension regulators, while men are the disciplinarians, providers and decision makers. The traditional male role is challenged by stepfamily life, for example, when money comes into the family from another man, or goes out of the family to another family, when decisions concerning the children and discipline in the family are not under the stepfather's control. However, men as stepfathers seem not to experience the same degree of distress and loss of certainty as women do as stepmothers, probably because they are not expected by society to be as involved with the care of children. Even if they do take an active part in caring for the children, it is their choice to do so, not their socially prescribed role. For stepmothers to accept that their role with their stepchildren will not fully replicate a mothering role is extremely difficult and they may experience symptoms similar to those in depressive illness – low self-esteem, anxiety, guilt, feelings of inadequacy, rejection and anger about it all.

Two clinicians, Morrison and Thompson-Guppy (1985), came to the conclusion that the stepmothers they were meeting in their practices were not clinically depressed, but were experiencing distress which is normal in the context of the adjustment required of them as stepmothers, and they described it as 'Cinderella's Stepmother Syndrome'. In a sample of twenty-two cases, selected because the help requested was for problems connected with stepmothering or stepfamily tensions, Morrison and Thompson-Guppy found that all the women were competent and experienced satisfaction in other areas of their lives, but felt helpless in their role as stepmothers, and most expressed fears that their 'inadequacy' meant that they were turning into the wicked stepmother. Yet they showed sensitivity towards their stepchildren and concern to care for their needs.

Most of them avoided blaming the stepchildren for problems imposed on themselves as stepmothers, and tried their best to substitute the maternal figures, without having much expectation of the stepchildren or being able to discipline them. Clearly, they felt they had all the responsibilities, but no rights. If they wished the stepchild were away – the only solution they saw at times – they felt as if they had actually rejected the stepchild. Due to the guilt feelings involved they often did more for the stepchildren than for their own. They came for help, often on their own, to try to be the 'perfect mother', hoping that they alone could correct the behaviour problems of the stepchildren seen by them. They wondered if they did not cause some of the problems as the impression they received from their spouse and from the stepchildren was that *they themselves* [italics mine] were the only problems. If they were not upset, everything would be fine. Though these women could well see that their husbands were often siding with the children and excluding the stepmothers from decision-making and discipline issues, their anger at their husbands was offset by the positive feelings they had in their marriage apart from issues concerning the stepchildren. . . .Also. . .they felt that if they complained or asserted themselves, their husband would reject them and they might even deserve it because they were not loving enough toward the stepchildren. (*ibid.* p. 525)

The role a stepmother assumes in the emotional life of the stepfamily is more demanding than a stepfather's. A man's commitment to the relational aspects of the home and family is partial; a woman's is total (Marianne Walters, personal communication 1988). The stress a stepmother experiences when things go wrong causes her to evaluate herself as a 'failed person' in the most important part of her life, as one whose identity in the world is faulty, or 'spoiled', an expression the sociologist Erving Goffman (1963) uses to describe the effects of social labelling. Many women's sense of failure follows them for years, even when the partnership is strong and survives and the family is integrated. Even when stepchildren are grown up and intimate ties exist and are valued, a stepmother can feel she failed to be a 'perfect mother', especially when there are differences between her feelings for her stepchildren and her feelings for her own children.

Here is a stepmother looking back on her experiences after many years:

'I made it very clear I was their stepmother. I respected their mother's right to be remembered. But after my children were born it got more complicated. Sometimes. . .I think I took out

> my frustrations with my stepchildren on my own. I would not
> smack another person's child, but I could punish my own
> because I could cuddle them very quickly afterward. . . .I have
> to say that my feelings for my stepchildren are not the same as
> for my own. Maybe they don't all know the difference, but it is
> different. . . .What does worry me is that I was not sympathetic
> to them [when they were children] in the same ways I was to
> my own, for example, when they were ill. I could not fuss over
> them. I was concerned [as I am now] but not protective in the
> same ways I was with my own.'

These are the words of another stepmother whose children
and stepchildren are still young. Her stepchildren live with her
and their mother lives in another country:

> 'I heard my stepson on the 'phone to his mother say to her, "I
> love you", and it hurt so much! You think you've come to
> terms with the whole situation, and then some tiny thing can
> make you feel completely thrown out again, after [several]
> years. . . .There is no automatic right of caring or receiving
> care back from your stepmother. She is here only for this time
> and purpose. Your mother's your mother forever.'

To be a stepmother who is not a replacement mother, but is
nevertheless a positive and significant person in a child's life
carrying out the functions of a mother, is quite a feat. Both the
stepmothers whose words I have just quoted assumed full-time
care of children whose mothers had chosen a completely
different life, one which did not conform to the cultural image
of the ideal mother; in abandoning the role, they abandoned
their children also. As a result, both these stepmothers had to
care for children who needed a great deal of reassurance about
their worth as people, like many children who are in foster care.
But stepmothers do not see themselves as foster mothers, doing
a caring job, they see themselves as 'mother' and require of
themselves a mother's capacities.

Motherhood is a natural vocation for many women, but it is a
questionable assumption that it is natural for all women, or that
every woman wants babies. We can and must challenge the
notion that a woman who does not want babies or does not
enjoy motherhood is an unnatural woman. Some women love
their children but do not enjoy spending all day alone with
them. Some men are better at relating to small children than are
many women. But society has institutionalised motherhood and

made it the first imperative for women, and has imposed a style of motherhood which is intolerable for many, and perhaps for all women under certain circumstances (Barnard, 1975). One such circumstance, arguably, is stepmotherhood. Barnard cites studies which show that maternal warmth is related to life style, and is at its lowest under conditions of crowding and isolation. Stepmothers, as we have seen, experience isolation; stepfamilies are often large families with too little space for all the members. She also says – and I believe this to be applicable to the stepfamily: 'Maternal instability was. . .found to be related to household composition and maternal obligations' (*ibid.* p. 37). The household composition of stepfamilies is complex and may fluctuate; the maternal obligations are ambiguous and contradictory. Listen to the words of this stepmother:

> 'Society's attitude toward stepmothers? As with mothers, basically, "seen and not heard", having to get on with the work and taking care of children – a huge responsibility which is given no recognition. Family and mother are held as very important, but [there is] no help in carrying out the tasks. The implication is that every woman can do it with no help, all alone, and that is put on stepmothers too, that all these skills are available overnight. The all-embracing mother, at the ready for anyone who comes along and needs a bit of nurturing. It is exhausting, it is debilitating, and no surprise to me that women become depressed and resentful of that situation. Stepmothers can fall right into the trap of doing this. When they do it they get enormous flak – from the ex-wife and, maybe, the partner. It is no-win. You have no rights, no basis. . . .Added to that, there is the enshrined nuclear family, held up as the ideal and "real" family we must take care of, and by implication we should be stamping out stepfamilies. So, it is as if the stepmother shouldn't really be there, the family shouldn't have split up, so she has to be ignored, and she is. And often [she is] doing an enormous amount in rearing children. And yet she survives, often at the expense of her own development.'

It seems that our cultural notion of ideal motherhood is always situated in the ideal family (that is, not in a stepfamily or a single-parent family) and in a set of ideal circumstances which is rarely to be found. These might include sufficient financial resources to ensure freedom from poverty, enough physical space to accommodate everyone comfortably, social supports to provide a network of approving and helpful people, a social environment that fosters personal self-esteem (there would, for example, be no racial or class prejudice), no physical illnesses or disabilities to contend with, and so on. On the other hand, it is also part of our cultural belief that the mother should be able to care unstintingly under any circumstances. Even when ideal circumstances do exist, as they may in, for example, a stable middle-class milieu, not all women feel fulfilled by motherhood. Many guiltily seek self-fulfilment in other areas or blame themselves for feeling depressed; they find they are unsatisfied and have a sense of being denied full participation in the adult world.

I remember a woman, not a stepmother, whom I met as a client in a Child and Family Guidance Clinic; she was a mother of two young children and had come because, she said, she was unable to deal with them. She was alternately impatient and irritable, then filled with guilt. Her doctor had given her tranquillisers and she was afraid of becoming addicted. She was a trained and experienced teacher of learning-disabled children who had given up her profession when her children were born and, of course, she felt her knowledge of children should have benefited her as a mother. She had never felt exasperated with the children she came in contact with in the course of her work as a teacher, and she wondered if her maternal instinct was lacking or somehow distorted. I asked her why she had given up work completely and she told me that both her family and her husband's advised it because it was best for the children, and her husband wished it also. She felt absolutely cornered and inadequate, 'in the wrong' *vis-à-vis* all the people most important to her. The more they did to 'help' the more undermined and angry she became. When she showed anger, her husband would often ask if she had taken her tablets instead of asking her why she felt angry. She was sensitive to her children and they were healthy and lively, but the price she was paying was very high. She was certainly not self-fulfilled.

What are the implications if we admit that motherhood does not provide total self-fulfilment for all women, and that some women, perhaps large numbers, will make other choices for their lives and possibly fit child-rearing into a career, or even choose not to have children? Can we accept that mothers have feelings of both love and hate towards their children? Was the idea of mother love, perfect mother love, invented in order to deny that women do have ambivalent feelings towards their children and that these feelings are just a natural reaction to taking on the enormous responsibility of another life? Was it invented in order to keep women economically dependent and prevent their having an equal say in making decisions?

We know that the notion of ideal motherhood which we have inherited in the West is about 200 years old (Badinter, 1981). Sometime in the eighteenth century the ideal of mother love – of the mother sacrificing herself for her child – began to have an impact. Badinter traces its historical development in France, where changes in attitude towards children and child health arose in the second half of the eighteenth century and changed women's lives. Prior to that time, in the seventeenth and early eighteenth centuries, women expected to send their children to be nursed by wet nurses, and this practice was by no means exclusive to the wealthy. It was believed to be preferable for both infants and mothers. No woman expected all her children to live. It is even argued by some writers that less affection was invested in children, at least until they had survived the dangerous period of infancy. In any case, women did not choose to devote themselves to infant care, to the exclusion of all other activities, if a choice were available, and they were not condemned for this until, in Badinter's analysis, about the time the 'back to nature' philosophy of Rousseau took hold. Women then were urged to breastfeed their children themselves and to keep their children with them and under their supervision. Thus, philosophers, doctors and – later – Freud, began the process of laying the responsibility for the physical and psychological health of the race on mothers, and this gave rise to the notion of motherhood as an institution, and to the guilt that went with it.

Badinter quotes an eighteenth-century writer, Prost de Royer, who, when exhorting women not to use nurses, said that only the mother would have the instinct, that innate, unconscious knowledge, to care for her child. Badinter says that in de Royer's view, and that of his contemporaries,

the stepmother and the nurse were considered incapable of loving the children for whom they had 'accidently' been given responsibility. Since their instinct would not urge them on, they rarely experienced – it was said – affection for those unwanted burdens. The stepmother was supposed to feel even less than the nurse, in fact, since traditionally she was the personification of the 'bad mother'. It was assumed she felt only annoyance toward children who were not her own. In a way, her hateful nature was actually reassuring [to this philosophy], establishing as it did a strong contrast with the good and affectionate mother. The mother-stepmother duality created order in nature and emotions, which explains why the stepmother was long considered the Other, the false mother. But confusion and disorder would emerge once the natural mother was characterised as possessing the same negative traits as the stepmother. (*ibid.* p. 160)

Any ambivalence must therefore be denied.

It took time for the notion that a woman should dedicate herself to the care of her child to become established. 'The "woman" disappeared behind the "good mother", whose responsibilities extended further and further' (*ibid.* p. 173) but only slowly; it took about 100 years. At the end of this long process it came to be believed that every woman, unless she were deviant or unnatural, or not the child's mother, had the right instincts. It became unthinkable – an aberration of the natural – for a mother to have both loving and resentful feelings towards children or, more precisely, towards the overwhelming responsibility of being a mother. During the process fathers were gradually relieved of responsibility for their children. In previous centuries a father had been held responsible for his child's misdeeds; now it was the mother.

'There have always been mothers but motherhood was invented' (Dally, 1982, p. 17). Two hundred years of idealisation has brought motherhood to a crisis. Today, more stepmothers than ever are faced with their special dilemma: how to be the perfect, loving mother when you are the stepmother – the other. Wives and women may be less idealised than they were 100 years ago, but mothers are more important than ever. Society accepts divorce, albeit reluctantly, as a fact of contemporary life, but the family which can result from divorce, the stepfamily, sits very uncomfortably on the social conscience. Society puts stepmothers in the same hallowed place as 'mothers', while simultaneously holding them in suspicion as culprits.

'Mothers bear the burden not only as child-rearers but as scapegoats' (*ibid.* p. 18). When things go wrong with children or with families she is blamed, but she is left to carry out her crucial tasks with few organisational supports. 'Motherhood' is a loaded term. The stepmother's burden as scapegoat is even heavier than the mother's. She epitomises the failure of the ideal mother; she embodies the negative feelings about caring for children and bringing them up successfully; she symbolises the end of a first, nuclear family.

It is time we developed and acknowledged a different set of expectations pertaining to women as mothers, and that we redefined our ideas about stepmothers. Of course mothering is important to women, and many have the necessary qualities and skills to be good at it without sacrificing other qualities and skills. Some women find their entire source of self-fulfilment in mothering not only their children, but other people's as well, and many stepmothers find joy and satisfaction in bringing up stepchildren. What I am suggesting is that more stepmothers would find their role more satisfying and less stressful if it were defined differently; if they were, perhaps, a sponsor for the child, a sponsor in the world for their partner's children and not a 'mother', with all the contradictory and impossible expectations that involves.

Listen to this voice:

'My stepchildren live with us and I don't have children of my own. I try to fulfil a mother role without displacing their mother. They are my routine, my purpose, my domestic life. . . .I must admit I'd never really thought of myself as a stepmother. It's a hard word. Nasty things are conjured up. [The children] are just part of [my partner] and part of the situation. My role is to look after them; I say to other people that they are not my children and that I look after them. But I am a typical mum in what I do. I ask about homework, bend their ear about bedrooms. . .they are my responsibility, just as they are [their father's]. I must admit I don't like to think of myself as stepmother, but they are my life. I don't want to compete with their mother. . .[and] I don't want people to make mistaken assumptions. They [the children] would resent that more. . . .[To another stepmother] I would say, "Give of yourself but don't expect too much back, because you never get back what you really want. Be a little distant because there is a lot of hurt, a lot you don't know. Let them be themselves. . . . You need to sort out a lot with your partner or there will be friction. You've got to be someone the kids will like as you are. If you try to be perfect, the strain on you will make you break. . . .Be your partner's partner. Expect to get hurt,

because it happens, and be a little wary. Don't think you can
cope with anything at all. You do have to be very, very giving.'

Not all stepmothers live with their stepchildren. It is
sometimes argued that there is less ambiguity for part-time
stepmothers and less stress. My conclusion is that this is not so,
and that part-time stepmothers experience much the same
difficulties. The stepmothers whose words are set out below are
ones whose stepchildren visit:

'I would say. . .don't try too hard. Think about how to explain
it. I tried to be this perfect – whatever, whoever? I didn't know
what I was and then I went the other way and distanced myself.
Now we are in a more comfortable, settled phase.'

A second said:

'My advice is, forgive yourself, and worry less about what all
the other people think, – family and others. Everyone expects
you to be the mother in some way.'

And a third:

'What you do together is what links you to your stepchildren, is
all that links you; you have no legal link, no biological one, no
history. That's something to say to stepmothers – find a task,
because since you don't know each other, and you both are
afraid, you do less and less together. It's like having to create a
way that a relationship can begin to define itself and become
special to those two people, to have some kind of meaning,
because there are no meanings or rules other than ones that
don't apply, except to hate each other, and to be afraid.'

PART II

The stepmother and the family

CHAPTER FOUR

'You are not my real mother!'

He turned away, which said more than words could do, but he had used words too. He had asked me why I kept changing things. I was making a new flower bed, but it meant something quite different to him. I was changing his mother's garden.

A stepmother

Children can be defiant or they can be sad when they say, 'You are not my real mother!' They can say it, or their behaviour can express it even more clearly, in a thousand little ways. You are driving the car and in the car are your stepchildren and your partner. The children do not speak to you; they ask their father about the journey and its destination although you organised it. You are all having a meal together; the children ask their father to pass them things, as if you were not there. You are having a meal together. You cooked it, but they will not eat it. It is as if they are saying, 'I can only accept food from my real mother.' Your stepchild is injured or ill, but ignores your offer of comfort, as if saying, 'I can only accept comfort from my real mother.' To accept comfort or food, or anything at all from you, is to accept your presence, your presence in their mother's place.

When a stepmother is confronted with 'you are not my real mother' it is a moment of crisis. Both she and the child are faced with the insecurity of their relationship to each other and its awful hazards of rejection and uncertainty. The stepmother is rejected as a parent and may not have imagined any other possible role she could play with her stepchild. The child is exposed to adult anger and resentment. Each is alone but they are caught up together in mutual exclusion. The discomfort they feel is heightened by their being caught together as if they were both children, needing to be given guidance and direction, and both feeling alone and frightened. A moment of crisis happens when there are no existing methods to solve a problem, or when previous methods are no longer effective; it is an adaptational challenge. A stepmother will be very fortunate if she has a ready-made method for dealing with the challenge being described here.

The challenge usually arises when the stepmother is attempting to exercise authority over the child. That is when the message 'you are not my real mother' is most overt. One stepmother told me:

> 'There was a moment, very early on, when I had to caution one of the children to be careful, not to do something, and he shouted back at me, "You are not my mother – you can't tell me what to do!" [I persisted]. . .almost immediately afterward he came and sat close to me. He had somehow worked it out in his own mind, and I said to him, "I promised your mother I would look after you all the time. I've got to look after you." '

This stepmother could act as she did because she had known the children's mother. As she said,

> 'It was a bonus for me that their mother and I were great friends first off. I could say this to the children. . . .but to them she was an angel, absent angel. Nothing you can do can live up to that idealised memory they have of their mother.'

In spite of that unfair comparison, this stepmother had a way to cross the gulf, because her role had a degree of clarity: she was there to keep the children safe.

Most stepmothers plunge into a controlling, disciplining role with their stepchildren in an effort to dispel some of the confusion about who and what they are. Read Delia Ephron's 'Notes on Stepmothering' in her book, *Funny Sauce* (1982), for example. She describes what happened the first time she was alone with her future stepchildren. They climbed into a fountain, but one which was dry. She told them to get out.

> Naturally they refused to obey me. But more was at stake here and we all knew it – our futures. Lisa and Alex were seizing an opportunity themselves: They were taking a stand against me, the intruder. It is one of the few moments in their lives when they have been in agreement. And I, in my muddleheaded way, continued to insist. (p. 159)

Six years later she muses:

> In the beginning there was the fountain and the fountain had no water

in it, and I told Lisa and Alex to get out. How absurd. Not that the
fountain was empty, but that my first word as their future stepmother
was 'no'. This little detail sums up the dumbness of stepmotherhood,
or at least my approach to it. A mother begins with 'yes'. The baby is
hungry. The mother feeds it. The baby cries. The mommy picks it
up. The baby needs changing. Yes, yes, yes. The mommy builds the
love and trust. Then one day the baby picks up an ashtray and starts to
bean itself. 'No', says the mother, and takes the ashtray away. But I
started by seizing the ashtray. Under these circumstances, it's a
miracle that the love came at all. (pp. 181–2)

I have been struck by the fact that virtually all of the
stepmothers I interviewed, plus the stepmothers I have met in
my clinical practice and those I know informally, have
expressed a view of their partner's parenting which is critical. I
have to declare that I am no exception. In the early years I was
convinced that I was the parent who could put everything right,
if only my parenting position were acknowledged. I would be
clear, consistent and firm. It seemed obvious to me that the
tensions increased when my husband was present; my stepson
became more demanding of his father and ignored me, or asked
his father something he had already asked me, ignoring
whatever I had previously said. As I reflect now, I think my
stepson was more able to accept my presence when he did not
have to see me as part of his father, the part his mother had
been. It took years for him to accept the partnership between his
father and me, and for me to become a familiar and accepted
presence in his life. During the years of feeling excluded and
resented, especially the first one or two, I relieved my feelings
by criticising my husband's parenting style. 'Leave it to me; I
can do it better, or if not, you do it better yourself', was my
implied message. It was arrogant of me, and insensitive, but I
was using the only evidence available to me, the change in
atmosphere that made itself felt when both my husband and I
were present with my stepson. Another stepmother, looking
back over many years, said to me:

**'Funnily enough, it was best when [the father] was away. As
soon as he was in the house there were conflicts and jealousies.
[My stepdaughter] wanted to look after him, used to say she
wanted to stay at home to look after him, without me being
around.'**

A couple, who both have children from previous marriages and
are trying very hard to be aware of all the issues, described to

me their critical views of each other as parents, (she thinks he is
not firm enough; he thinks she is too harsh), and the
heightening of tension in the family when they are both present.
'When I am on my own with them, they are more relaxed, and
they do as I tell them', she said. 'It is easier when [their
stepmother] isn't there', he said.

This is the way Delia Ephron describes it:

> She [the stepdaughter] wants him [the father] to change his mind; I
> listen, convinced, even panicked, that he will; and then, he does. . . .
> This brings me to the stepmother's most important function from her
> point of view, and her most dispensable from everyone else's:
> criticising. Though she would describe it as 'seeing things clearly'
> . . . .Because she is a stepmother and, again her own words, 'not
> involved', she can't help notice her husband's little failures as a father.
> Naturally, she is nearly driven crazy by what she sees. Oh, the
> frustration of it, having to stand by and just watch. Of course, she
> wants to be helpful. So she points out to her husband how he is
> 'letting his child down' and expects him to shape up. . . . 'It's not
> good for Lisa to have a daddy who reneges on the limits he has set,' I
> say to Larry the second Lisa leaves the room, and sometimes before,
> which drives Lisa mad. 'It's not your business!' she screams at me.
> But doesn't she understand? It's my duty to interfere, for her
> sake. . . .I am utterly convinced that, were I the child's mother, I
> would never change my mind once it was made up. (Since I am not
> the child's mother, I am safe from ever finding out I'm wrong.) I
> regularly compliment myself with the thought, I'm much tougher
> than Larry is, and when given the opportunity I always prove I am.
> (Of course, I am – I'm the stepmother and not involved.) Right is on
> my side. Parents should set limits and stick to them – all psychologists
> agree with me. . . .It doesn't temper my zealousness or make me
> more understanding to know that many divorced fathers are too
> indulgent, and there are reasons for it. I even know the reasons.
> [Guilt, compensation, easier to be nice than tough, anxiety about
> discipline, inexperience as a disciplinarian.] Being reluctant or too
> insecure to discipline your child is a sad situation to be in, but I am not
> saddened by it because I am too busy trying to do something about
> it. . . .Why can't I shut up about it? No parent wants an unbiased
> observer in the house watching him. That is truly a parent's
> nightmare. . . .And no one but a stepmother would think that a
> stepmother is unbiased. (*ibid.* p. 165–7)

Here is one couple's problem:

**'The main problem was and still is, to some extent, that when I
felt that the children should be handled in a certain way and
insisted on it, my husband felt undermined and inadequate as a
parent and "sulked". I felt the same [i.e., undermined and**

inadequate] because he wouldn't take my "advice". We're still working on that one! One of the disagreements that we had was that I felt he was too soft with his daughter. He felt that she had suffered more over the departure of their mother. She consequently managed to wrap him round her little finger and I found myself, quite often, in the role of the wicked stepmother. We talked it over and he agreed to take on the disciplining of his children more often. As a result I was able to let go more and be softer and kinder towards them. I also had to learn to admit to myself that I was "a bit" jealous and try to overcome that.'

Obviously the two need to agree on discipline, or she needs to relinquish her criticism of him as a disciplinarian, so that the opportunity exists for her to create a warmer relationship with her stepchildren. I think this stepmother's recognition that she was not really unbiased helped her to do this. Another woman had this to say:

'We [the stepmother and father] are in agreement on the broader issues of their upbringing but differ on day-to-day matters. The difference between a parent and a stepparent, in my experience, is that parents are infinitely more tolerant of their children than stepparents are! It's hard to remember, but I think I have always wanted to impose more rules and structures than my partner thought necessary. When they were young I regarded the children as unruly and difficult to correct, whereas my partner regarded them as free and spontaneous! I have always had some difficulty in finding an appropriate role. I have always felt rather redundant to them – they have never been lacking in love and attention from either parent and at the beginning there seemed to be no role for me to slip into.'

Except the critic? She now has children of her own, and says:

'My attachment to my [children] is much more emotional – intense and passionate. I have more patience with them and feel more responsible for their upbringing. I feel more in control of their lives. . . .My stepchildren never wanted an intense relationship with me, as they had with their own parents. . .I do think, however, that I lacked patience with the children at times when they were small and that I was intolerant of my partner's level of commitment towards them.'

A third woman would have liked more support from her husband.

'He [the husband] did not expect me to take over like a mother. He expected me to be friendly, have a good relationship with his son, and that is all really. . . .We usually agree about the

children, but I have felt critical of his indulgence of [her
stepson], like not asking him to help out in simple ways. . . .[or
not correcting him]. When he comes in he ignores me, or
rather, doesn't respond to me. When I put his food in front of
him he might say, "Oh, Mum makes a better spaghetti
bolognaise than you do!" I would like his father to take him
aside and talk about that sort of thing. He never does that, but
he knows; he is afraid that if everything does not go well for his
child, the child won't want to come back. The visits have to be
perfect.'

A fourth woman said:

'One of the things that was an issue was discipline – I
disapproved of some of the things [the stepdaughter] did and
wanted to indicate that. I discovered that. . .too many adults
were telling her what to do. Also I felt like a guest for a long
time and so would keep quiet when I disapproved.'

Things resolved themselves to some degree when this stepmother and her partner moved to their own house, where the
stepmother established some rules which apply when her
stepdaughter is present, but she described to me how much she
has learned in the intervening time about the flexibility which is
needed to deal with children and her criticism of her partner has
subsequently lessened. She has been helped by experience, but
significantly, also by having a clearer role and greater control.

In case I seem to be saying that it is part-time stepmothers
without children of their own who are critical of their partner,
let me make it clear that some of the women whose words I
have just cited are full-time stepmothers with children, and the
following one is also:

'Her father and I did not agree – he just said that all I did was
nag. It caused much trouble between the two of us. He never
disciplined her, never structured her. I tried to, but the more he
did nothing, the more I nagged. At dinner, for example, I
thought the children could clear the table. I worked all day and
made dinner and they were old enough. But [the father] would
get up and clear the table instead of asking her to do it, because
he was afraid I would have an argument with her. . . .She
always knew when her father was coming, and her behaviour
would immediately change.'

But part-time stepmothers are more prone to feeling excluded
and unnecessary. What can they provide that the child needs?
What they do provide is advice to the father about what the

child needs. The result can be disastrous – mutual blaming between the couple:

> 'In theory we were in agreement [about handling and disciplining the children] but the reality was that I had brought up a family and [he] had separated from his ex-wife when his daughter was five. He was reluctant and incapable of disciplining her. He was unsure about the effect – would she want to see him? This led to a burden and restriction on me. If I always wielded the "heavy hand" she wouldn't come to see us and I would be responsible.'

This part-time stepmother is almost in despair:

> 'We are never in agreement about the [step]children and never were. If I mention [extra work or behaviour issues] he says I don't want the children there. It's just not true. He won't discuss it, or says I'm always going on at them. He thinks only he should tell them off, but he never does. I feel unsure about my natural reactions to their behaviour because their father doesn't trust my natural reactions. If he supported me I would feel easier, infinitely easier. . . .He refers to them as his children, excluding me. I know there is a lot of guilt for him, but he blames me for it. I have always wanted the best for them [the stepchildren]. But sometimes what I see as best is not the same as what my husband sees as best. He doubts my motives, I think. For him, whatever I do seems wrong or not enough. He wanted me to fit into his life with his children and not make demands of my own. . . .I don't feel guilty about not having the same feelings [for my stepchildren as for my own child] but I do in the context of having been too hard in the beginning, expecting too much.'

At a very early stage the combination of the stepmother's expectations with the father's guilt about the end of his marriage to the children's mother caused a breach between this couple. Now their relationship is full of mutual recrimination and empty of efforts to reach each other through openness and communication.

Parents who part have difficulty explaining to children about ending their marriage. The painful changes involved, the guilt about the children, the sense of failure and the uncertainty about the future all create enormous inadequacy in every parent who has ever experienced them. To explain the death of a parent is equally difficult, but cannot be evaded. Research into the effects of divorce upon children indicates that explanations help children to come to terms with the changes, and to accept other changes which follow, but are notably lacking at the time of separation and divorce (Walczak and Burns, 1984). Perhaps the problem is that where divorce (and remarriage) are concerned, children are most in need of explanations at a time when parents are least able to give them, unless they have guidance from someone outside the situation or are fortunate enough to know what the children require and are emotionally able to provide it. What the children need is to be talked to and made to feel involved in the feelings and forces which are shaping their lives. Parents often feel helpless; they do not know what to say to their children. They imagine they must find the correct words and phrases and end up saying little or nothing. Walczak and Burns quote a child who said: 'but the fact that we talked about it makes it easier' (*ibid.* p. 100). When a stepmother enters the scene, she is frequently blamed by the children for their parents' separation, whether she was a feature of it or not. The intensity of the children's resentment of her is the stronger because of the inadequate explanation from their two parents about their separation. As this stepmother comments:

> **'You get the situation where the stepmother is seen as having broken up the parents' marriage. I reckon that most parents don't go out of their way to let the kids know that it is something wrong with their relationship that made them part. In my situation, I know that both parents were happy to let the kids assume it was my fault. I think it may be easier for a lot of people to blame an outsider rather than take the burden of responsibility themselves, at least where the kids are concerned.'**

When a child says in either words or behaviour, 'You are not my real mother', this may be a plea for an explanation. 'You are not my real mother, and what does that mean?' It may be a cry of pain. 'You are not my real mother, and where is she? Why am I abandoned?' It may be a burst of anger. 'You are not my real mother and I will not pretend you are. I will not be controlled by you, or cared for by you.' It certainly is a statement of loyalty. 'You are not my real mother and I will remain true to her.' An adolescent boy said to his stepmother: 'I don't owe you anything. And it was my house first.' This was a statement of loyalty to his mother and to the previous family unit. The stepmother was devastated by the hostility, of course, which she had done nothing to deserve except to be there, the symbol of changes which the boy did not want in his life. As another stepmother said, 'I am not the reason their marriage ended but still I was "the other woman" for a long time. . .I felt everyone hated me. I felt mean – we all got mean!' She went on to say:

> 'I think what helped me with my feelings of hatred was to acknowledge them, and not say I didn't have them, but to own up to them. They are part of me and, yes, part of being a stepmother and of being a child myself who didn't get all I needed. . . .To accept that there are good and bad feelings and. . .allowing both kinds of feelings to be. One of the liberating things for me which helped me to begin to love my stepchildren was when I found out it wasn't just me, that other people I loved and trusted had the same struggles, that I wasn't inherently evil. When I stopped putting all the bad intent in the child and accepted my bad intent, her efforts to wind me up became just that and nothing more.'

As stepmothers struggle to find meaning in their role and ways to exercise it, they often make surprising discoveries. It was a surprise to me to find that in some families it is precisely because the stepmother is not the 'real' mother that she can provide some of the explanations a child needs. She cannot hurry that; it takes time – time for her own jealousy to subside and become protectiveness, time for her to become familiar and predictable to the child. Listen to this voice:

> 'My main concern – and that of both parents – was that the children should not feel torn or resentful. So my aim at the start was to stay in the background, making no demands upon the children. I let my relationship with the children develop at their pace – slowly! – and was forever dreading any sign of rejection. . . .I have always had some difficulty in finding an appropriate role. . .always felt rather redundant to them [as] they have never been lacking in love and attention from either parent. [My stepson] saw me as someone he could talk to on the subject of his parent's marriage and divorce. They [the children] have always desperately wanted their parents to be reunited. The "civilised" nature of the marital breakdown and of all the parents' dealings with each other thereafter meant that the children could never understand, or remember, what had gone wrong. They maintained a fantasy of their parents reuniting for many years, notwithstanding the obviously important place of myself in their father's life.'

Another stepmother said:

'It isn't so much that I am afraid the kids will leave me, but that they really don't need me in their lives. I rarely go to them but I wait for them to come to me. I wait for their overtures. They don't come to me out of love as they do for their father, but because I am a friend. I do sometimes step into the breach. . . and give more attention and also take their part. One of the functions, I think. . .is to be a kind of advocate for them.'

And a third:

'I was thinking how much I shut myself out. I seem to gain some firm ground from time to time and then move forward. Recently I took a big step by going to pick up my stepdaughter from her mother. I'd always avoided it, and this time I went alone, and I was able to talk with her. I felt a part of something which includes her. . . .The stepmothering bit now feels firm. . . .Being able to enable people to develop, to respect a child's individuality, that kind of enabling, seems a lot of what being a stepmother is about.'

A fourth stepmother said:

'But the good part of our relationship is that he sees me as the person who explains. . . .He asks me what his family means, about what would happen if his father should die. He told his mother about what I answered and the result is that she has now made a will and so has [his father]. [My stepson] knows about it.'

A stepparent can have a kind of objectivity that is hardly possible for a parent, and maybe children with both a mother and stepmother can experience a dimension of mothering which is very positive and adds to their lives rather than threatening their loyalties by competition with their mother. But, for this to happen, clearly the mother and stepmother must come to terms with each other's existence so that the children can allow the stepmother to have a place in their lives.

Here is a stepmother whose stepdaughters are young adults:

'One of them was quite hostile in the beginning. . .although I felt sympathetic to their situation and was not surprised at any hostility, I nonetheless did not care to be the target of their anger which they had difficulty directing towards their father . . .he simply put me ahead of them. That initial period did not last very long, probably because I made no strong attempt to make them like me or accept me. . . .I did feel badly for them, and one of them. . .started seeking me out as her confidante . . . .I am glad that my relationship with both of them is now

pleasant, and that I can be supportive of them. They are both
fond of me, and try to be supportive of me in family
controversies.'

And this voice:

'Maybe one of the liberating aspects of being a stepmother is
that you can consider motherhood without the constraints of
the institution of motherhood. You don't have to give uncon-
ditionally, control every breath in an effort to get something
back. . .you have the possibility of loving without the beastly
emptying of trying to 'mother'. I can remember one day. . .
that I suddenly realised I do have love for these children.'

And so, when the cry goes up, 'You are not my real mother' a
response might be, 'That is so, and we can make the most of it.'
It is possible for a stepmother to build a relationship with a
stepchild which enables each of them to settle into a new family
situation and gain security and identity from it without
displacing the child's mother, without trying to be the 'real'
mother. What is a 'real' mother, if we leave aside the biological
relation? One definition of 'real' is genuine and, therefore, the
woman who gives birth is without doubt a genuine mother.
However, many people who are adopted say their adoptive
mother is their 'real' mother, that they know they have a
biological mother but do not have a sense of belonging to that
mother. Stepchildren too, can have a psychological link with a
stepmother which is strong and not ambivalent and some, as
adults, describe having been cared for by both a mother and
stepmother and claim to have close and deep ties with both.
One stepmother I talked with said she felt she had 'psychologically adopted' her stepson, and another said she knew she
'felt right in the right places' about her stepson and that she was
his 'real' mother, although he carried inside him the memory of
the mother who gave him birth.

In trying to understand the meaning of these complexities I
studied a report by Margaret Draughon (1975) in which she
discusses three ways, or models, for stepmothers to become
identified with their stepchildren. There are two basic assumptions implicit in this study. The first is that the stepmothering
role is permanent and stable, unlike the temporary role of a
nurse or foster mother. The second is that the stepchild is old
enough to be aware of separation from the biological mother.

Draughon says that a six-month-old child can experience feelings of permanence and, therefore, can experience loss and grief when people and things change. The three models stepmothers might choose from are related to the needs of the child; another way to express this is to ask what changes the child is mourning and how that influences the stepmother's choice of model. For example, a young child who lives all the time with father and stepmother is dependent on the stepmother both emotionally and physically for 'primary' mothering – especially if the child's mother is no longer living. It is as if the stepmother were the only mother. That is complete dependency, and there are degrees of dependency upon the stepmother, which Draughon's three models embody. The first is 'attempting to become the *only* or "primary" mother, i.e., psychologically supplanting the biological mother' (*ibid.* p. 185), while the second is attempting to become an alternative or 'second mother' to a child. The third – being, or trying to be, a 'friend' to the child, not a mother figure at all – is not about dependency upon the stepmother for physical or psychological survival. It is about being a part of each other's life in a very significant way, but the two may or may not be close and intimate in their manner of relating.

If a child's mother is dead, the child will mourn the loss of that loved person on whom he or she was most dependent, and while the mourning continues, the mother is, as Draughon puts it, 'psychologically alive' to the child. The grieving process – talking about mother, missing her, being sad – needs to be encouraged by those who are caring for the child – the father, perhaps grandparents or foster parents, or a stepmother. A young child who is allowed to grieve for a dead or absent mother, will eventually be receptive to a substitute, the stepmother. Such a stepmother is unlikely to hear 'You are not my real mother' from her stepchild after the period of missing and grieving has passed. By relating to a stepchild in a way that accords with the stage of mourning the child is in, a stepmother can help the child towards better adjustment and, in the process, clarify her own thoughts about her role.

It is equally relevant, when the mother is still living, to find an appropriate basis for the stepmother relationship through the child's need to mourn. How might a stepmother do this? As stated before, although the mother is living, the child grieves for the first family structure, where earliest needs were met and where earliest consciousness resides. Draughon suggests that the stepmother should find out how much contact the stepchild has with the biological mother in order to assess the need or desire of the child to have a replacement mother. Age is obviously also an important determinant. Young children provide opportunities to talk about change by asking questions; they will demonstrate their need for comfort and reassurance by demanding attention or by becoming withdrawn. In the early stages, the stepmother may be rejected when she tries to respond. For the child, especially the older child, whose mother is 'physically *alive* and present to the child, [she] would probably also be psychologically alive and, therefore, *not being mourned* by the child' (*ibid.* p. 187). Stepchildren in that situation may be sad at times, perhaps confused and angry, but only in relation to the lost family structure, not to a lost mother. The stepmother who attempts to replace the psychologically and physically alive mother and become the 'primary' mother, or even an 'alternative, second mother', will meet resistance and probably hostility. She will probably hear 'You are not my real mother' in several versions, even though the children are likely to be dependent on adults for some years to come. A better model is the 'friend', which does not challenge or injure the child's image of his or her mother, and which allows the child's sad (and angry) feelings to exist and to abate at whatever pace is needed in order to accept the changes. The stepmothers I talked with whose stepchildren ask them for explanations about their family, marriages ending, parents separating, or parents dying are using the 'friend' model. They are acting as trusted adults and they are nurturing a child just as surely as a mother does, but in a different fashion.

Many of the stepmothers in the group I interviewed said they are, or want to be, a special 'friend' to their stepchildren, and were exploring how to do this on a 'trial-and-error' basis. One of the exceptions to the 'friend' model said that she thought she had become a 'psychological' mother to the younger of her two stepsons although his mother is living and he feels affection for her. The mother is not a stranger to him; he had contact with her during his childhood and adolescent years, but received little from her in terms of his needs for care and dependency. His stepmother supplied those needs from his early childhood, and it is to her that he relates with warmth and intimacy. With her older stepson the relationship is different; he had stronger memories of his mother. Using Draughon's concept, his need to mourn her and the loss of his first family were greater. Indeed, it is possible that his mourning was never completed. His relationship with his stepmother is distant and difficult. This is how she described it:

> **'The aim we had – looking back – was that we would be a lovely, normal family. . . .The younger child was withdrawn and distressed and we concentrated on him – and I now think to the deteriment of the older one, who was a very angry and unhappy little boy.'**

I think it is likely that the father and stepmother helped the younger child, who was easier to get close to, through his mourning period, while the older one remained confused and isolated. This stepmother grieves over the loss of her own ideal of family life:

> **'Then there was a blow-up which showed me it was not OK, my "careful" stepfamily, and. . .I felt that my whole family had fallen to pieces – just awful grief – I saw for the first time that I had kidded myself, that we had never been a family that was "good enough" and that there was this hatred [from the older stepson about the ending of his parent's marriage]. What I am facing now is that the image of family life we thought we had we actually didn't. . . .I always blame myself – must have been something I could have done better or did wrong. I make excuses for them but never for myself. I want to get it right – for him, but also for his father. But I would say [to the other stepmothers], don't pretend to pass "as if", which we certainly did. . . .Rituals expose everyone to pretence, like wills, weddings, funerals. . . .Stepchildren suffer from being different, the loyalty issues, and it is about unresolved grief.'**

Draughon closes her paper by noting that her second model, that of being a 'second mother' to a child with the result that a child has two mothers at one time, does not seem beneficial under any of the conditions she has considered, yet it might possibly be the most common choice of identification for stepmothers. I would suggest that most stepmothers have not perceived that there is a choice, as I said in the last chapter, and are trying to have a 'lovely, normal family'. It is also possible that the 'friend' model seems limited and difficult to maintain when it comes to issues of control and discipline. The 'friend' model is the only reasonable choice, however, when the stepchild's mother is alive and present in his or her life. Circumstances under which a stepmother becomes the 'primary' mother to a stepchild will be relatively rare. But in every instance of stepmothering, in the early stages, the stepchild will need the stepmother's acceptance of his or her grief about the changes in family life. The degree and intensity of grief will vary from one child to another, however, depending on such factors as the amount of time between the end of the first family and the beginning of the stepfamily, the degree of understanding the child has about the changes and the personalities of all those involved. No stepmother I talked with – whether full- or part-time, and regardless of the ages of the children or participation of the father, regardless, too, of whether the stepmother welcomed the child into her life – said that the beginning was easy or problem-free.

Here are the words of a stepmother who assumed full-time care of a little boy of seven:

> '**I wanted to make up to him for previous painful experiences. I wanted to make his life happy. I was in a new life with a future – never dreamt it could exist! How could I be so lucky? "Seventh Heaven" included the child. . .but he was very difficult. He was clingy, then tantrums, then clingy again. His mother had left very abruptly, but he didn't appear to be shattered; instead he became very withdrawn. . . .I felt I was succeeding with him after about a year. . . .the only problem [after several years] is disciplining. That is better now as I have learned not to interfere [when father is disciplining]. . . .I think of myself as his mother – the mother role. I know I am not a second-best mother, because I am a better mother to him than his own. . . .He never refers to me [outside the family] as his stepmother, though he kids me about being his "wicked stepmother".**'

Is that this boy's way of saying, 'You are not my real mother'? It may be his way of acknowledging the relationship, but she described an affectionate tease, not a challenge or a cry of pain. In this stepmother's story, what I hear is that she and the child's father helped and contained the child through a period of intense grief, and that now, while he is perfectly aware of her relationship to him, she is his 'psychological mother'. His own mother is living, but not alive inside him as the mother who cares for him and nurtures him.

My conclusion is that the 'real' mother is the one who is psychologically alive to the child. Usually this is the biological mother or an adoptive mother, but in some circumstances it can be the stepmother, or some other person, such as a grandmother or a foster mother. I would add that being the 'psychological mother' cannot be imposed or competed for and that the stepmother's alternative, being a friend, is not less or more than being a mother, but is something parallel, something important and essential in a child's life, although harder to define. Friendship between a child and adult not only takes time to develop, but will involve elements of direction and control as well as guidance, which friendship between two people of the same age will not. Friendship between a stepmother and stepchild, however, if it takes root and grows, will be permanent. 'Friend': one who is not a foe, one of the same nation, party, or kin; one who is 'a favorer; a promoter'. The word comes from an Anglo Saxon verb, *fréond*, meaning to love (*Webster's Collegiate Dictionary*, 5th edition, 1948).

CHAPTER FIVE

The outsider as insider

You can feel like an outsider – not counting. We were talking with some other members of the family about what would happen in the event of their parents' deaths, and I found I was not considered for my stepdaughters. . . .You do all this and then it comes to nothing. The payoff is that you don't have to take all the responsibility, but it is strange – a relationship where there is closeness but no kind of public sanctioning.

Yes, I am an outsider and I have to be, but I get pulled in, or allow myself to be pulled in. It is true I give them something extra, in addition to their parents, and outside the responsibility for their whole lives.

I have felt sort of abandoned sometimes, when I realise they can remember things and talk about things in the past that I know nothing about. Then I see that my stepson feels abandoned too, when he sees the closeness and affection between his father and me.

Three stepmothers

A stepmother is both an outsider and an insider. As the partner to the father of children she is an insider, she has knowledge and information about intimate matters concerning her partner and his children. She is an outsider because her rights and responsibilities are not clear to herself or the other intimates, and possibly not acknowledged by important people. In the first stages, it may be only the stepmother's partner who acknowledges her membership in the family unit. Others are not extending it, or only tentatively. Over time, the stepmother's outside position changes to one of greater familiarity, at least, and perhaps to greater clarity and acceptance. She may never feel a total insider and, for some stepmothers, partial membership works best. For others, there is a degree of sadness about it even after many years. This chapter is about the different ways stepmothers adapt and about family membership and changes in family membership.

An outsider is someone who does not have full membership in the group, or institution or, in this case, family. It is only a stepfamily or, perhaps, foster family, which we could speak of as having partial members. In nuclear families, whether or not all members are pleased to be in each other's company, there is clarity about membership; members are bound together by their relationship to one another by marriage, birth or adoption (Carter and McGoldrick, 1980). The boundary of membership in stepfamilies is not clear, perhaps not even agreed upon by all those who might have a share. In addition, the boundary of the stepfamily has to be elastic, or permeable, in order to allow members to come and go, sometimes belonging to one unit in one household, and sometimes to another, as children do who visit one parent and live with the other.

It is possible to have a legitimate claim to membership but still feel like an outsider, not sure of one's place in the group, one's rights, responsibilities or privileges. This is where stepmothers begin. 'I look after the children, but I have no authority', is a statement often heard from them. 'I feel doomed never to be allowed full membership in the club' writes Delia Ephron (1982, p. 162). Another voice, a stepmother trying to find ways to make partial membership work, says:

> 'I am there in their home and they are there in my life. I help with homework and go shopping for them, and with them. I prepare food for them. I think about them and I'm concerned about them, but I cannot control their behaviour. I have no legitimate authority. I can tease them into changing behaviour, but I cannot direct them. Their father disciplines and sets standards. When he is out I sometimes withdraw if they misbehave and leave them to it.'

The most emotionally painful outside position is to have no legitimate authority and, in addition, to be outside the closeness between others, like this stepmother: 'It's always "his" children, and they come first. He refers to them as "his" children in a way which excludes me.'

There is a kind of loneliness in stepfamilies from which no member is immune – feelings of being bereft and excluded, of being a stranger, of being powerless to change anything and jealous of closeness and ties between other members. Jealousy is a word often used when stepfamily matters are discussed. Because it has pejorative overtones I want to make the use of the word in the context of this book as clear as possible. The father mentioned in the last quoted statement appears to be jealous; that is, he is possessive about his children, and he seems to see the stepmother as a rival. Jealousy in this instance means possessive intolerance of rivalry, the desire on the part of one person for another's exclusive affection. But jealousy can also mean apprehensive fear of rivalry; a person can imagine that if affection grows between others it will result in his or her being excluded or displaced. The father referred to above could be afraid of losing his children's affection or having it diluted. The stepmother could be said to be jealous of the bond her husband has with her stepchildren because she feels shut out by it and disregarded. The following definition fits this stepmother's position, and that of most of the stepmothers I interviewed: 'Jealousy – feeling aggrieved or excluded by a loved one's relationship with another as being prior to or of greater importance than one's own relationship' (Christopher Beedell, personal communication, Jan. 1989). A slight variation of this fits children in stepfamilies for whom jealousy means feeling aggrieved, excluded and displaced by a new relationship of one's parent which appears to have greater importance than one's own with that parent. Therefore, in relation to step-families, we must say that jealousy is always at least a three-person issue and means that there is a feeling of fear at a given time on the part of one person that the other two (or more) will shut out the one, and this fear may well include anger.

In the context of the stepfamily, the concept of jealousy does not refer to destructive, irrational suspicion and distrust, but to the fear of being excluded together with *a lack of confidence as to membership*. This is not irrational fear and it is by no means only the stepmother who is afflicted with it. Children whose parent establishes a new partnership with another adult, a stranger to them initially, treat that stranger as an outsider, and they may react with jealousy; it would be exceptional if they did not, since they are outsiders to the new relationship between the two adults. The parent who perceives tension and distance between the children and the new partner experiences loneliness coupled with confusion, and may withdraw temporarily, or even permanently, and make no effort to reduce the tensions or bridge the gap. Sometimes the parent will react protectively, shielding the children from the stepparent's hostility and thereby increasing it. Alternatively, the parent may react with possessiveness, jealously guarding closeness with the children which often becomes very strong during the phase of single parenthood. The new partner, realising that the attachment between the children and their parent predates the attachment between the couple, feels lonely, unneeded, resentful and jealous. Supposing that the parent who does not live with the children remains in contact, that person watches a new family forming around his or her children and former partner, and also feels lonely – acutely so when he or she had not wanted the first family to break up. Well-defined boundaries of intimacy that once existed are now shifting; new partners share sexual intimacy and the minutiae of daily life; new adults have a place in the family constellation.

The question of who belongs to the family when a stepfamily comes together cannot be answered by simply describing the members of a household. Some members of the family live together all of the time while others may be visiting members, as when children spend weekends and holidays with one or other parent. The children and their parent are closely connected and may have a deep affection for one another, but they do not live together. The children may have feelings of not actually belonging in the household; the stepparent may have feelings of being an intruder in their own home when their stepchildren are present. It is a more complicated matter than where parents, children and stepparents live. None of the members know how they should relate to one another, and all are burdened with conflicting emotions. There are, of course, complexities of family formation when two people who have never married before come together, but those complexities are socially and publicly familiar. Expectations as to roles are reasonably clear and prescribed, at least within culturally specific norms. In-laws may or may not approve of or like one another, but they know what their relationship is to the new couple. As to the new couple – most of us hope to like our partner's family, but few of us expect to love them. Society does not expect us to love them;

indeed, jokes about in-laws help to relieve any guilt which might arise from not loving them, mother-in-law jokes being the classic example. Stepfamily relationships might be compared to in-law relationships because stepchildren are, in a similar sense, one's partner's family. Yet, while society does not expect stepchildren to love a stepmother – in fact, hating her is sanctioned – paradoxically, people expect that love will spring up instantly in a stepfamily and, especially, that the stepmother will love her stepchildren.

When a couple separates and forms new partnerships, there is much greater confusion about liking, loving, or simply accepting the changes than there was the first time around. A warm relationship with a former mother-in-law can become painfully strained or be lost; one's membership in a family where one was once accepted may be discontinued and will certainly become ambiguous; grandparents who once played their role with confidence and pleasure can become estranged from their grandchildren, not knowing how to function as outsiders to the new family which includes their grandchildren. They may be excluded from contact with their grandchildren because of conflict which preceded the separation of the parents, or for some other reason. Grandparents also suffer because of social expectations – should they be able to love their stepgrand-children from the word 'go'? Other members of the wider family – cousins, aunts, brothers or sisters of former partners – also become outsiders. Everyone's role is in flux, everyone's basis for relating to everyone else is in question. One colloquial definition of 'family' is that it is 'the place where when you knock on the door they have to let you in'. A stepfamily might be suspicious of the person who is knocking and wonder whether to let him or her in.

Grandparents can play a decisive role in helping a stepmother to become, or hindering her from becoming, effective and confident. This stepmother is talking about grandparents. The set she lives nearest are biological grandparents to her two stepchildren, to her child by her present partnership, and stepgrandparents to her three children from a previous marriage. She says:

'They [have been] no help whatsoever; possibly a hindrance in that they expect [me] to be a full-on twenty-four-hours-a-day,

**seven-days-a-week mother to their grandchildren, but THEY
can't extend themselves to be full-on grandparents to children
that aren't naturally theirs. They display obvious distinctions,
giving to one and not the other – the excuse is that they're old.'**

Perhaps it is unreasonable to expect grandparents to accept
grandchildren who are not 'naturally theirs', but it is easy to see
how discrimination of the kind this stepmother describes
hinders integration in a stepfamily and keeps some of the
children outsiders when others are in. In this stepfamily all of
the children live together in one household.

Another family, also one in which all of the children – five of
them – live in one household, provided still another perspective
on the issue of grandparents. In this stepfamily, the father is the
parent at home; he is the one who is there when his three
children and two stepchildren come in from school. The
mother/stepmother works full time at her profession. They say
they are both 'stepmothers' since he is the parent who does the
housework, takes the forgotten items to school, listens to
reports of the day and does all the many other things the full-
time parent at home does. One grandparent was very disapproving, not only of the stepfamily, but of the man's electing
to be the parent at home while the woman is employed, and that
grandparent is estranged from the family. Another set of
grandparents – and there are four sets – has welcomed the
children, all of them, but there were problems:

> **'We made a mistake there early on, [because] this set of
> grandparents had all the children visit at once, trying to make
> no distinction, and we found that was resented by the two
> whose grandparents they are. Now they go to visit on their own
> sometimes. It is not always fair to be fair! Kids want to be
> special to their grandparents. There are two other sets – one is in
> touch and available and visits us, and another has contact with
> the children when they visit their mother. . . .[Their chance to
> be special.]. . .The children get jumpy at criticism they hear
> from grandparents. One child heard [her mother] described in
> denigrating terms by one of them. . . .We don't need that
> aggravation!'**

In the whole range of grandparents available to this family,
some have been supportive and non-judgmental and others have
not. When grandparents are judgmental they can cause a lot of
harm, saying things to the children about their parents and

stepparents which are upsetting and undermining. The experience of hearing a parent criticised by a grandparent is similar to that of hearing an absent parent denigrated by the other parent and stepparent; for the child it is like hearing a part of him- or herself run down and criticised. If the adults are not able to negotiate these matters, the grandparents are at risk of being excluded and the children of missing out on relationships which are one of childhood's riches. Of this family the father/ stepfather said: 'One set of grandparents have compensated for the loss of others; they have become the family grandparents. I feel fortunate [that the children] all have the experience of loving grandparents.' In the first example above, three of the children have not had that experience; they have remained outsiders. None of the other possible sets of grandparents in the family are available because they are either too far away or are not living.

If grandparents have a degree of choice about including stepchildren in family membership, and families about including grandparents, stepmothers do not have such a choice. They embark on stepmotherhood with only one clear expectation, and that is unrealistic: to love the stepchild instantly (Visher and Visher, 1979). It is one of the myths which have an impact on stepfamily formation; another is that stepfamily integration takes place quickly, and still another is that a stepfamily can duplicate a biological family (*ibid.*). These myths help to maintain a stepmother's sense of being an outsider and of being under scrutiny, of having to prove membership of a family by succeeding to do the impossible. As this stepmother said:

'When you become a stepmother, there is an assumption – made by the father, the extended family, family friends, teachers, neighbours – that you will love the child and provide what is needed and is missing. There is also a kind of watching to see how you manage; maybe you will turn out to be a classic stepmother. I began to realise that I was failing to love my stepson and I thought I had become the wicked stepmother – or worse, that I had been a bad person all along. The only person, a friend, who ever talked to me about it told me I didn't have to love him, but I had to be kind. By that time it was too late because I wasn't kind.'

The comments of another stepmother are apt here:

'I think stepmothers need a warning about how intense the emotions can be in a stepfamily. The bottling-up may start

with the shock of that intensity. How much anger and frustration there is. . .it's the most common experience, but stepmothers feel ashamed of it. As a result a child can be seen as the whole problem, or the child's father. . . .Totally illogical. Why should you love some child you don't know? Yet we all have this fantasy that we can all do it.'

A stepmother enters the stepfamily with her fantasy, with unequal parental authority and, possibly, with little support from any source. As her level of stress rises her self-esteem is certain to fall. Women with no source of personal satisfaction outside the family are especially subject to crippling stress. Even with such satisfaction, if her partner is unsupportive, the stepmother will be distressed.

A study of stepmothers came to the conclusions that the psychological stress they experience arises because they are expected to perform their role effectively with too little support either from within the stepfamily or from society; because their own personal needs are largely unacknowledged and unsatisfied and because they suffer from low self-esteem due to a lack of confirmation that their efforts as a stepmother are appreciated or valued. This is the stepmother as outsider. But for many stepmothers things do improve as they feel a greater sense of belonging. Time and satisfaction gained from other sources, such as a strong relationship with a partner, heal and restore confidence. Here is a stepmother talking about her stepson, a little boy who spends weekends with her:

'He gives me resentful vibes when I tell him off, whereas with [my own child] ten minutes later we are OK. He bears a grudge. It is harder work, but. . .you must have some rules in the house for all the children. It is beginning to feel natural and good in its own way – less confusing.'

This stepmother is gradually achieving a workable relationship with her stepchild as a result of being consistent and insistent, and because there is an agreed policy with the child's father. She also describes experiences she has shared with the child which were relaxed and pleasurable, outings and special meals, for example, when the father was in charge of any necessary control and she could concentrate on building a friendship with a small boy. There is a level of shared parenting and open communication which is moving the family towards 'feeling natural and good in its own way'.

As women and men share family responsibilities more equally, as fathers become more actively involved in the care of their children, as women become freer to act and express themselves independently and to seek self-fulfilment outside the family, there is a chance that stepmothering will become less stressful. However, social change is a slow and difficult process; the old ways and old ideals remain in place, albeit less firmly. Even with changes in roles and expectations, stepfamilies will have initial difficulties to negotiate, overcome and accept. It takes time to make the transition from outsider to insider.

All families, stepfamilies included, develop in stages, but because of their different starting point, stepfamilies have their own stages and pace of development. A first family begins with a couple to which children are added; the family adapts gradually to the changing requirements of all its members. When a new member is added to the family, a baby, profound change occurs, but the change will have been signalled well in advance. Each person has a new dimension added to his or her identity: the couple become parents, the woman becomes a mother, the man a father, a daughter becomes a sister, a son becomes a brother, and so on. The changes may be challenging but, in a first family, there will have been time to prepare for them. If the addition to the family is an elderly parent, the chances are still that there will have been time to prepare for his or her arrival in the household. Then there is an event – such as death or abrupt family break-up – which brings about sudden change; the members of the family have to adapt quickly. Everyone's usual way of managing, relating and coping with daily living, is disrupted, and there is loss – loss of the deeply familiar, loss of a loved person, loss of the predictable patterns everyone is accustomed to. There is generally a more gradual build-up to divorce or separation but whatever the changes they may bring – the end of incessant and unresolved conflict, hope for some, hurt for others, grief for all – they bring uncertainty. A stepfamily begins its life with most of its members feeling pain in connection with the past and all feeling uncertain about the future with, probably, little or no preparation for coping with the gains and losses.

When two people unite to form a first family, they bring many kinds of expectation with them which will be fulfilled or modified as the two learn to live together. When two people become partners and one, or both, has children of a previous family, the scene has more players. After the break-up of a first family, the children live with one parent and, if the other parent is living and available, visit that parent. Relationships between a lone parent and his or her children often become close and intense as the parent turns to the children for emotional support; this can occur with both the custodial and non-custodial parent. This closeness has been described by some writers in such terms as 'pathologically intensified' (Fast and Cain, 1966), 'intense overdependence' (Messinger and Hansen, 1976) and 'exceptionally close' (Visher and Visher, 1979), the implication being that such closeness is always harmful. This is not so by any means, although when it becomes too intense it can prevent new relationships from forming and lead to dysfunction in both adult and child. At its most extreme, it can turn into a sexual relationship, which would, of course, seriously harm the child. Leaving aside such pathological closeness, the family structure of single parent and child has potential positives, for example, when children are allowed to assume appropriate responsibilities and enjoy a status which enhances the maturing process and minimises adolescent struggles for independence (Marianne Walters, conference on Mothers and Daughters, London, 1982). The relationship between a child and one parent is obviously different from that between a child and two parents living together. The two adults will share family responsibilities and probably rely more upon each other than upon a child for emotional support. A stepfamily appears to replicate a two-parent family until we remember that there is a third adult somewhere who, as the child's other parent, has much influence over the family.

The different circumstances for the development of the stepfamily have been observed and described by Patricia Papernow, a family therapist and researcher. She has identified seven stages of normal family development (Papernow, 1984). She analysed the information gained from lengthy interviews with stepparents, then tested the conclusions on many more members of stepfamilies and discussed her findings with other professionals who are involved with stepfamilies, such as teachers, lawyers, and the clergy. Papernow's stages follow one another chronologically, and progression from one to the next depends upon a degree of success in meeting the challenges of the previous stage (*ibid.* p. 357). For example, the first stage is called 'fantasy'; various dreams, hopes and wishes are held by both adults and children about the stepfamily. Adults have fantasies about rescuing each other and the children from a sad past, about healing the hurt from the past – and this might include a determination to provide protection from a previous partner. Both parent and stepparent have fantasies that the children will welcome a stepparent, either as a knight in shining armour or a perfect mother. The biological parent will usually cling to the fantasy that this time he or she has found a partner with whom life's burdens can truly be shared. The adults' fantasies are about correcting the past or even obliterating it, whereas the children's are about returning to the past and 'correcting' the present – reuniting their two parents or, at least, making the new adult, the stranger, disappear. They may even have fantasies that things will be worse than they actually turn out to be. Obviously, as the family progresses to the next stage as a result of living together, fantasies must change and be allowed to disappear. If fantasy is not relinquished the family will remain gripped by a kind of paralysis and not be able to move successfully to the next stage of development. The process of creating the trust and nurturing atmosphere which characterises a family which is valued by all its members, whatever type of family it may be, cannot take place in an atmosphere of fantasy. But Papernow warns that the fantasy phase must be respected by people outside the family, such as counsellors, friends and relatives. It is unhelpful to try to disabuse people of their fantasies too abruptly; gentleness and understanding are needed. The phase will pass in its own time and most people, says Papernow, look back upon this phase with embarrassment and even a degree of shame.

In the case of children whose parents separate and form new partnerships, a fantasy phase can recur, or a new one can arise. An adult who grew up in a stepfamily told me of the fantasy he had when a little boy; it was that his father, the parent he did not live with, would have a new family and 'forget all about my brother and me'. Many children describe fantasies which are actually fears. These may occur later on in the life of the stepfamily. For example, if their parent and stepparent have

normal arguments, the children become frightened there will be
another separation, another painful and bewildering change.

The second stage in the cycle is called 'assimilation'. This
occurs when the stepparent has become familiar and, perhaps,
accepted, but is still an outsider to the intimacy between the
children and their parent. The 'new family' is still forming; it
has not become firm and accepted by everyone. Two adults
have expressed their intention to join together, the act of joining
has taken place (formally or informally) and now the long
process of trying to build lasting relationships and a sense of
belonging together is under way. The firmly established
relationships between parent and children continue and the
stepparent feels left out and confused. It is usually some
recurring daily issue, such as who sits where when watching
television, that brings matters to a head. When there is a greater
sense that something is wrong and must be changed, stage
three, 'awareness', has been reached. There is seldom a blinding
flash of recognition, rather the gradual realisation that the
uncomfortable feelings of resentment, jealousy, exclusion and
conflict have an origin somewhere. The stepmother, at this
stage, is aware of a need for change but she does not know what
the change should be.

> 'I knew something was wrong. I felt guilty about resenting a
> child and then I resented [my partner] because he didn't notice
> that I was having trouble with my stepson. He just wanted me
> to fit in and be normal – in his house with his son. Then I felt
> guilty about being unhappy because, really, we had so much
> going for us. Finally, I realised it wasn't just that I was
> inadequate. Something had to change besides me.'

This stepmother describes the progression through the stages
of fantasy, assimilation and awareness. Her stepdaughter lives
with her mother and has regular contact with her father and
stepmother.

> 'One of the very early fantasies was that I could be happy to have
> her live with us if that should become necessary, and all would
> be rosy. Now I'm more sane and cautious and realise what that
> would mean. I would have tumbled right into it and I can see
> what problems there would have been. . . .Maybe she [the
> stepdaughter] transferred her wish and fantasy to live in a house
> where there was both a mummy and a daddy again to us, and

that may have been why her mother felt threatened and why
she refused to have me see [the stepdaughter] for a while. . . .
There have been ructions – very early on. I was the reason
[because I was the living symbol of the permanence of the
separation]. The mother pointed out that access was to [the
father], not me. I felt pushed aside, left out, and it was a shock
to my rather closed view of my relationship with him. I was
pushed aside for something that had been going on for longer.
At that time I hadn't realised the importance of access and
keeping to regular arrangements. I support that completely
now, but I refused to be left out of the visits, as the mother at
first insisted. I decided that some nonsense was going on, and
that I would not be left out.'

This stepmother felt left out for more than a year before
deciding to do something about it. Notice all the fantasies that
were going on in the beginning: the stepmother's that she could
create an instant new family for her stepdaughter, the child's
that she might 'live in a house with both a mummy and a daddy
again' and the mother's that the stepmother would steal her
daughter.

These first three stages – fantasy, assimilation and awareness –
form a group which Papernow calls the 'Early Stages' of the
stepfamily cycle of development. There are four more steps
which form the 'Middle' and 'Later Stages'. Families vary
widely in the length of time they take to progress through the
cycle, but Papernow points out that no family she studied took
less than four years. Seven years was the average period of time
and some families remained stuck in the 'Early Stages' after as
long as eight or twelve years, with divorce resulting in a
number of the families which were 'stuck'. One family she
studied in depth moved on to the 'Middle Stages' after nine
years together and appeared to be moving successfully through
the cycle at the time the article was written (*ibid.* p. 357).
Families vary in the amount of time they require to progress
from one stage to the next, and furthermore, they do not always
move forward evenly; a move back may be necessary before
moving forward again. For example, a couple might, at the
stage of 'awareness', move back to 'assimilation', and spend a
year or more establishing a strong bond between them before
they move on to work together in a parenting manner. Their
relationship is still new and has to withstand an onslaught from
others who both fear and resent its existence.

In the 'Middle Stages', consisting of 'mobilisation' and 'action', the family is restructuring to accommodate the changes which were felt in the 'Early Stages'. This can be a period of conflict when 'highly charged differences become aired for the first time' (*ibid.* p. 359). It is usually the stepparent who is pressing for changes in order to become a more equal partner and member of the family. Much negotiation, often involving arguments, is needed to bring about changes in areas such as contact with former partners, money to former partners, discipline, contact with children who visit, space in the house, and so on. Partners who have few conflicts in other aspects of their relationship find that their sense of dissatisfaction with each other over issues like these is difficult to resolve. They may continue to have conflicts over stepfamily issues for a long time while nevertheless finding fulfilment in each other as partners. When the two begin to take decisions together and to agree on the moves which need to be made in order to find some workable solutions, they are nearing the end of the acute 'outsider' period. The family can now mobilise itself to meet the needs of all the members in a way which can bring at least a degree of satisfaction to each one. What precedes this, and is necessary in order to achieve it, can be very distressing – especially so for a stepmother without children of her own. She will have been feeling isolated, unsupported and without a meaningful role in the family. In order for her to begin to be an 'insider', changes have to come about. She must be drawn into the family and acknowledged as someone important and permanent who has contributions of her own to make. Those changes will come about little by little over months and probably years.

The 'Later Stages' are characterised by greater intimacy; everyone is confident of family membership, the stresses of the outside world can be shared, there is predictability and acceptance and limits, too, in terms of demands. Some of the ways of the previous family groups will have been incorporated into the new family styles and ways and rituals. The stepfamily has become itself, a defined unit, involved now in its own cycle of development. Each individual member, whether child or adult, is progressing in his or her life, with membership of the stepfamily as part of that person's life setting. Papernow found that there was a wide variation in the ways that stepparents acquire a firm role in the stepfamily, but she did find they had some points in common. These are that the stepparent does not compete with the biological parent of the same sex to be the better parent, or try to replace that parent; that the stepparent is able to be an adult in relation to the children, that is, is not like another child under the direction of the biological parent; the rest of the family accepts the stepparent's role and position; and that the stepparent is able to bring his or her own special qualities to bear (*ibid.* p. 361).

Papernow was not focusing on stepmothers, but if I now do that, using her lens, I see that stepmothers find many unique ways to create and participate in family intimacy. One stepmother becomes the trusted confidante of her stepchildren, another creates new dimensions of activity for her stepchild, like this one:

> 'One way my stepdaughter and I got together was to draw a cartoon together. She was one character and I the other. It went on and on. In our cartoon drawing we went places together, and I would say, "Shall we go in this house?" and things like that, and she could tell me where we were by what she drew and what she wanted to do.'

Another stepmother described her long struggle against the intrusion of her partner's former wife. Until her partner recognised the need to limit the amount of contact his former wife had, until the new couple shared the struggle and acted together, the stepmother continued to feel excluded and somehow guilty. Yet another said:

> 'We have never tried to create a traditional family, or pretend that we were. . . .But we still have had, and do have, great difficulties. Preparing and planning does not eliminate them. [But it] makes it possible in the first place to acknowledge difficulties without blame or guilt. There still are painful times, problems over access to the other parents, times when the past intrudes most painfully. Times when you feel bitter and condemning of the ex-partner, the other parent, and you know it hurts the children to hear criticisms of their other parent, but you do not know what to do with your feelings. Or how to explain to the children when there is criticism. . . .No matter how hard we try to do things in the best interests of each member of the family, there is the going out and coming back and what happens when they are away cannot be controlled. There are elements of their lives that we can't help them with and we can't control for them.'

The stepmother in the last excerpt is explaining very clearly and cogently that she and her partner have achieved intimacy in their stepfamily and within the steprelationships. As a couple they share the issues, including the painful ones; each has a role which is clear and sanctioned by the other, and they have reached a stage in the cycle of stepfamily development which Papernow calls 'resolution'. The stepfamily is stable; few of the issues still require constant attention. Problems have been resolved by accepting what is and what isn't. Children are shared and the going away and returning always have some element of difficulty. One parent always has to accept the loss of day-to-day life with children; the other parent has to facilitate contact even when there is tension; a stepparent who has come to enjoy and value the children has to relinquish them and know, as one stepmother put it, that 'However good you are, you are not the real mother, inside them.'

The stepmother's compensation when this stage is reached is a relationship of trust with her stepchildren. She has a place which is meaningful to them and to herself. In Papernow's words,

> [she] is now solidly established as an 'intimate outsider' – intimate enough for children to confide in, and outside enough to share in areas which might prove too threatening to bring up with biological parents. Stepparents may now find themselves a special confidante to stepchildren in areas such as sex, peer relationships, drugs, distress that a biological parent is holding on too tightly during visitations, and unresolved grief about the divorce. (*ibid.* p. 361)

The outsider becomes an insider by degrees and, to some extent, always remains partially an outsider. Stepmothering, when its limits are accepted, can offer some unique satisfactions – the affection, confidence and companionship of a child without the burden of total responsibility – being a kind of sponsor, as durable and reliable as a parent but with more flexibility, more scope for adapting as the child becomes adult. There is more than enough evidence available to confirm this can be so. I heard it from many of the stepmothers I talked with, and there are other studies besides Papernow's to support it. For instance, Patricia Lutz (1983) examined stepfamilies from the perspective of adolescents. Her conclusions suggest that the longer a stepfamily exists, the less stress there will be, and that after it has progressed beyond the period Papernow calls the 'Early Stages', it is not very different from other families in terms of stress levels. Stress and strain are an inescapable part of family life, as are the good things which come with intimacy and belonging. As children grow up and parents grow older, stepfamilies – like any other kind of family – have to adjust to change and face new challenges. But they have many extra adjustments to make too. The ones the stepmother is able to make are of central importance, crucial to her own satisfaction and to the life of the family.

CHAPTER SIX

Where differentness is acceptable

She is not my mother – she's somebody special.

A stepchild

It is trust that we are working on. I hoped in the beginning I would come to feel the same about my stepchildren as I do my own. Now I am more realistic. It is strong but it is different.

A stepmother

Being different is often equated with being deviant or bad, having broken important rules, and most people do not want to be designated as deviant. Something has to happen before differentness becomes acceptable, unless we decide cynically that being different always divides people, and that to accept differentness is an impossible ideal. My conviction is that differences are an enriching part of life, not only acceptable, but important and fundamental to experience. Without differences, we would know little, and experience little; but difference and change are also threatening.

Stepmothering is not the same as mothering from birth. Stepfamilies are not the same as first families. The media attention which stepfamilies receive often reinforces the notion that they are not just different, but 'deviant' families, bad places for children to grow up in. We hear of children whose stepparents abuse them, of the numbers of children with stepparents who appear before the courts, of the bitterness children feel towards stepparents. No wonder many stepfamilies try to hide the fact that they are stepfamilies. What would convince them that it is good to be a stepfamily and different from a first family? The criterion of success for many such families is the extent to which they can hide the fact that they are a stepfamily, for to be different is to invite the suspicion that the family is unstable, or perhaps to invite unkind curiosity,

104

or a patronising interest with barely concealed condemnation. Children's surnames may be changed, adoption procedures may be undertaken, or other means used to hide the stepfamily status. Within the privacy of the family itself, certain subjects may become taboo; tension mounts when they come up; conflicts arise but go unresolved. For a member of the stepfamily to acknowledge differentness within it is to invite being excluded from family warmth and risk being unloved. For stepfamilies the fear of confronting differentness is 'normal' and to some degree is part of the early experience of every stepfamily. The stepfamily measures itself against the accepted model for 'family' and, in seeking the private satisfactions and public acceptance which pertain to the nuclear first family, often find that their private pasts intrude and spoil a public identity in the present.

For the stepmother the socially approved and idealised name of 'mother' is replaced by the reviled 'stepmother' label. The way she copes with the pressure upon her to win social approval and acceptance influences the family's view of itself. To the extent that she accepts the ambiguities of her role the tensions of the early phases will be less. This notion appears to put the major burden for the stepfamily's success on the stepmother; and while that may not be fair, the fact that the woman acts as the emotional pivot in a family means that it is true. However, it is only partially true. The stronger and more satisfying the couple's relationship, the better the chances it will survive the stresses of the early stages of stepfamily life. If they share the belief that the stepfamily status should be an open issue, the stepmother will at least have tacit support in her search for the meaning of her role. If the stepmother adopts a role model which is not the traditional one for women in families, and if her partner can vary the usual pattern for gender relations, they can avoid some of the greatest causes of tension. The stepmother would not then try to become 'like a mother' to her stepchildren. She would get to know them while the father provided the parenting – the discipline, probably much of the nurturing and, maybe, even the food. She would learn how much they needed and would accept from her, and how much she could provide. Most couples do not discuss the issues, however, but make assumptions about each other based on reactions to day-to-day occurrences. One stepmother, who expressed satisfaction in her relationship with her partner, said it had been very difficult to talk to him about the trouble she had in her stepmother role: 'He felt I was attacking his children, or attacking him, and he never knew whose side to take. When we could talk about the family from our being close as lovers it was less problematic.'

The stepmothers I interviewed varied in the kind and amount of sharing of stepfamily issues that they were able to have with their partners. Two of the thirty looked back on a separation which they saw as a direct result of a lack of sharing. One stepmother thought her job was made possible by the fact that she knew, and had been a friend of, her stepchildren's mother before the first marriage ended; she cared for this woman's children as a kind of trust. Another said that psychotherapy was the only thing that got her through the difficult years. Still another defined herself as a stepmother, yes, but a 'better mother' than the child's own, and claimed that is what sustained her when the child was very difficult and miserable. Of the women who were at an earlier stage in their stepmothering careers, one was close to ending her marriage because of the lack of understanding she felt her partner had for her position; another was discouraged but determined to survive. Many talked about another important factor which supports and sustains a stepmother: the friendships with other stepmothers, whose experience can form a point of comparison and reassurance. It helped them enormously to find out that they were not alone in having hateful feelings, and they said that the strength of the negative feelings was reduced, as well as the guilt about having them, when they were shared with trusted friends. 'Talking about both kinds of feelings [bad and good] allows them to be.' One stepmother said that more is needed than just becoming aware of, and admitting, feelings of anger. She thinks that

'people assume we are sort of tarnished and living with failure. So it isn't helpful for people just to say "Isn't it awful!" That seems to underline it. It is an enriching part of my life as well. I don't want to be dismissed with "Isn't it awful!"...There needs to be more than simply putting the balance right.'

There are, as she says, private satisfactions which are in contrast to the public image of stepmothering.

In order to gain the support of a partner, or of other women, a stepmother has to acknowledge first her status and then its effect upon her as an individual. In the initial phase of becoming a stepmother a woman is unlikely to want to discuss problems because of the fantasy surrounding this stage. Her desire to become part of the unit of father and children as quickly as possible is strong and tends to override any feelings of unease she may have. But when these feelings can no longer be ignored and the woman feels she is being shut out and rejected by the other members of the family, she might appeal to her partner. Evidence from researchers, clinicians and others (e.g., the National Stepfamily Association Telephone Counselling Service) suggests that stepmothers frequently feel unable to ask their partner for support, or that they do not try to do so because they believe it will not be forthcoming. They expect to be rebuffed – some may actually have been rebuffed and told 'it's all your fault' or that 'it's a woman's job anyhow'. It is likely that by the time a woman is aware, and acknowledging to herself, that she is having difficulties being a stepmother, she is already struggling with a loss of self-esteem, and she may actually believe that she is the problem and has failed to create the emotional climate everyone needs. Any attempt to share the problems with her partner is almost certain to result in less, not more, sharing, because she will appear to be 'attacking his children', as one of the stepmothers quoted above said. At this point, everyone is acutely aware of differences of all sorts: different levels of intimacy, different expectations of what life together would be like, different perceptions of what is happening, different ideas about how to achieve change and about what change is needed, different personal histories. Often it is a matter of luck whether or not a stepmother makes contact with a friend, counsellor or health-care worker who is sensitive and informed in stepfamily issues and can provide not only emotional support but a new perspective and a new definition of what is happening.

There are people – their numbers may even be increasing – who set out on their stepfamily life with the intention to be open with one another and deal with issues as they arise. I talked with one couple who have made striking efforts to be mutually supportive and to accept their differentness. Despite their efforts, they have not been entirely freed from stepfamily growing pains; at times they are perplexed, as all parents and stepparents are, struggling with baffling and unacceptable behaviour from children, or suffering from intrusion from former partners. Their approach, and their openness with each other has meant, however, that they rarely experience isolating feelings of guilt and frustration or blame each other. In my opinion, they have achieved an atmosphere of intimacy and trust in their stepfamily in a shorter time that would otherwise have been the case. Papernow found that the families who went through the developmental cycle fastest, that is, in about four years, were those in which the couple's relationship was an open one, with each partner supporting the other in his or her role as parent and stepparent. The couple I have just referred to had been together for six years when I interviewed them, and they spoke of four years as the minimum time it took for the family to develop and draw upon an atmosphere of intimacy and 'naturalness'. They had some other factors in their favour, factors which reduced the degree of differentness in their family: one was that both parents had children from a previous marriage. This meant that they each experienced what it was like to be a stepparent, and they were aware that this was an advantage; they started from the same place rather in the sense that couples do when they become parents for the first time. 'We can understand each other not only as stepparents but as parents.' In addition, all the children live in their household; neither of them is parenting the other's children on a full-time basis and their own on a part-time basis. The children all have contact with their other parent and, therefore: 'We both experience. . .the difficult times when we have to let the children go.' These factors have probably contributed to their more rapid development, and living with both children and stepchildren in one household has, no doubt, helped them come to terms with, and understand, the difference between the feelings one has towards stepchildren and those one has towards biological children – although they emphasise that they had the usual fantasies in the first stage of their family life that their feelings would be the same towards both sets of children. The myth of 'instant love' is a powerful one, and a universal one, for stepfamilies. As this stepmother said:

'We are very open [now] about not feeling the same about our stepchildren as we do our own. . . .[but] sometimes efforts to

**be fair make us more harsh with our own than with our
stepchildren. . . .juggling all of them, or trying to.'**

Being a stepmother can never be made easy. What we want to
know is more about how the problems arise and why in some
families they fade and in others the problems go on for years. In
an earlier chapter I mentioned the woman in her forties who
spoke of her stepmother almost as though she were a witch who
had come between her and her father over twenty years earlier
and stayed there. I do not know what other issues need to be
considered when analysing this bitter feeling. Was the stepdaughter totally unprepared for the advent of a stepmother? She
certainly was very nearly an adult at the time and did not need
'primary mothering'. Did the stepmother try to displace the
mother or eradicate her memory? She may have had a narrow
concept of family life which allowed for only one mother
'figure'. Was she really a dominating, insensitive person, or was
the father rather a weak one? Was he a prisoner or could he have
been allowing the stepmother to create a barrier which he
actually wanted? I am reminded of this quotation from Ugo
D'Ascia which Belotti (1975) uses:

> On the subject of the negative characters in fairy tales, he acutely
> remarks, 'Behind the wicked stepmothers, witches and ogresses in
> which fairy tales abound, there is always a weak man who is
> unloading all the most thankless tasks and decisions on to her'.
> (p. 102)

The woman I talked to, who blames her stepmother, would, of
course, not judge a loved father so harshly, but the loss of her
intimacy with him has remained a painful aspect of her entire
adult life. Surely the responsibility for the estrangement is his as
well, but the stepmother bears it all, at least within the
judgment of the stepdaughter.

In contrast, there is a man who spoke of his stepmother as 'the
stranger who raised me'. He said, 'She could have avoided
taking any interest in me, but she always did. She helped and
listened until the end.' For a stepmother to become acceptable to
a child, it seems that she must show a basic and demonstrable
intention to contribute in a positive way to his or her life and in
a manner appropriate to the needs and age of that child. In
addition, the father, the stepmother's partner, must acknowledge
the stepmother's benign intentions, and maintain his own

parental relationship with his children while she is establishing a relationship with them which may or may not be parental.

When stepchildren are young, under the age of 5 or 6, and live with the stepmother, she has an obvious role to play and the stepmother label may hardly seem relevant. The difference between such a family and a first family with small children may not be apparent – except to the various sets of grandparents – especially if the mother is not living or not in contact. Burgoyne and Clark (1984) describe a group of families like this. From the sample of forty families they devised a typology of five groups, none of which was very large, obviously, but each group, nevertheless, provided important information about the kinds of images of family life couples use when they embark upon stepfamily life. The first group, with young stepchildren, is called 'not really a stepfamily'; their life approximates more closely to that of 'just an ordinary family', especially if the couple add a child of their own and have no problems with previous partners. In such families the stepmother will become the 'primary' mother for the children. Unacceptable feelings of differentness may never make their appearance, although it would clearly be a mistake to mislead the children about the steprelationship. A child who discovers that the parent she or he believed was a biological parent is not 'real' feels dislocated and frightened. The child is reacting to the discovery of deception in a loved and trusted parent figure, not to the lack of a biological connection. A stepfamily cannot eradicate the fact that it is different from a first family by disguising the fact that it is a stepfamily, however simple or tempting that solution may seem. Nor should it assume that the fact is unimportant. I wonder, for example, whether stepchildren in Burgoyne and Clark's first group will need to challenge the 'ordinary family' myth when they are adolescents.

The second group in Burgoyne and Clark's typology also reflects the significance of age, or rather, the stage the first families had reached in their family life cycle when they ended and a new family was formed. The families in this group were those with older children of one or both partners, children who were adolescent at the time the stepfamily was created. There is a high level of turbulence in families with adolescent stepchildren, as there is in almost all families with adolescents, and for stepmothers who are not mothers in their own right, it is probably the most stressful situation of all. Couples in this group are often looking forward to the departure of the children so that they can have some time to themselves. For that reason, and because of their age, they are unlikely to add any children of their own and will not, therefore, establish 'ordinary family life'. Differences between this type of family and a first family with older children are very obvious. Nevertheless such families do often achieve family solidarity and the nourishment which flows from it. Of note is the fact that in this stepfamily type both partners are often already parents, and can thus understand each other's experience as both parent and stepparent.

Those families which appeared to accept their differentness and to look for ways to exploit it formed the third group, the 'progressive stepfamily'. They take a 'pluralistic' view of family life and

> are aware of a diversity of patterns in family and domestic life and depict themselves as making choices and responding to constraints in a way which would exploit the advantages of their circumstances for their children. (*ibid.* p. 193)

Although they may have young children from previous unions and be adding children, their expectations of family life are diverse and not tied to tradition or convention. In this group of seven couples, three included women who had not been previously married, and of the other four, both partners had children. The three women may have seen themselves as not conforming to conventional expectations and were therefore prepared to try to create a family unit that fell in with the pattern of the family they had taken on. The fact that the couples in this group did not expect to recreate an 'ordinary family' does not imply they did not have adjustment difficulties, but, 'where such difficulties persisted they were faced, resolved and controlled' (*ibid.* p. 193). There are two important factors common to most of the families in this group which undoubtedly help in resolving problems in stepfamilies: they had few persistent conflicts with former partners, and almost no financial problems. These advantages, together with an attitude towards family life which takes variation from tradition in its stride, appeared to make the fact of being different from other families irrelevant. One family did have financial concerns, however, so we must not conclude that ease of adjustment is simply a matter of being able to afford it. Financial problems in stepfamilies are usually, although not always, accompanied by unresolved conflicts with former partners and are thus a constant reminder of the past. Some stepfamilies – probably a minority – accept the past and, therefore, accept differences also.

The fourth and fifth groups in Burgoyne and Clark's study consist of families who were consciously pursuing 'ordinary' family life – one group doing this successfully, the other failing to do so. There were ten families in each of these groups. In both groups the stepparent was attempting to play a parental role in as full a manner as possible, but in the second group, efforts to do this were undermined or blocked by constant intrusions from the past. These came in the form of unresolved legal issues relating to the ending of previous marriages, and conflicts with non-custodial parents over access, custody or money. The desire to have a 'normal' family, with privacy and intimacy, was unmet; the family was subjected to judgment and scrutiny from outside, sometimes by professionals, such as social workers and solicitors, sometimes by extended family and neighbours. The first group – families 'largely successful' in the 'conscious pursuit of an ordinary family life together' (*ibid.* p. 193) – encountered the inevitable problems of the early stages of stepfamily life, but were able to overcome or ignore them. Both these groups of families took the attitude that different-ness was *not* acceptable and should, therefore, be ignored or eradicated as far as possible.

Ten years after the original Sheffield interviews had been carried out (but three years after Burgoyne and Clark's book was published), another researcher did a small follow-up study of one family in each of the groups in Burgoyne and Clark's typology (Batchelor, 1987). Her conclusions, which must remain somewhat speculative as they are based on one interview with each family, suggest that the typology holds, that is, that the couples continued to define their family life in the same way, drawing on the same images of family life as they did ten years ago. Batchelor says:

> If stepfamily success is seen in terms of the couple staying together and raising children to adulthood whilst maintaining an apparently satisfying couple relationship, then my original hypothesis that

stepfamilies can succeed has been confirmed. This success is achieved in the face of the many contradictory pressures stepfamilies are under: that is, to be the same as nuclear families *and* to be different. (Section 6, p. 1) [italics mine]

One couple which Batchelor reviewed had separated, and this was the couple from the group with a 'progressive', or alternative image for themselves, but they were continuing to act as co-operating parents, even to their stepchildren, and had every reason to consider themselves successful as the type of family they had wished to be. The stepmother in this case does not regard the stepfamily or her performance as a stepmother in terms of failure, although social norms and values no doubt would do so.

This book is about stepmothering and in this section I am asking whether the difference between the experience of being a stepmother and being a mother can become acceptable – to her and to the stepfamily she is part of. Like Batchelor's conclusions mine must be speculative also, based on single interviews, personal experience, and intuition, and not in any case, purporting to be social science. After considering the stages of development that a stepfamily goes through, and the various types of stepfamilies there are (the types being based on the images of family life which the culture provides), I do reach some conclusions. It seems to me that the more possibilities a woman can entertain for ways to relate to a stepchild other than as a mother figure, then – provided she enjoys a reasonable level of communication with her partner and manages to contain her sense of loneliness when communication breaks down from time to time – the more she will be able to tolerate the ambiguities and frustrations of stepmothering – and eventually she will discover its satisfactions.

It is important to consider once again the differences between stepmothering and other forms of substitute mothering because these differences make it significantly more difficult to find satisfaction in stepmothering. In common with adoption or fostering, stepmothering is about caring for someone else's child, but, it is not merely about caring for someone else's child, it is about caring for the child of one's partner, the child who was the result of a previous affection, a previous sexual bond. Unlike foster mothers, stepmothers have a tremendous emotional investment; they must get it right – for their partner and for themselves, first, and for the child, second. Foster mothers do not set out with any particular emotional investment, although the child comes first in their concern to 'get it right'. Adoptive mothers do have an emotional investment in the child they adopt, and need to prove to themselves and their partner that they are good mothers. The child comes first for them both. Adoption and fostering are sanctioned and admired forms of substitute mothering, and the differences between these forms of mothering and biological mothering are acknowledged and accepted from the beginning. Leaving aside (but recognising) the sadness infertility causes, we can state that an adoptive mother is 'different' in a socially acceptable way because she is assuming total responsibility for a child whose birth mother has given up that child, and she reasonably expects to become the psychological mother. The foster mother is also 'different' in an acceptable way; she never sets out to become the psychological mother, although she may do so at a later stage. The stepmother's differentness is not socially approved and may well not be acceptable to her in private. She may cherish the fantasy of becoming the child's psychological mother, even if the child is still firmly attached to the biological mother. Whatever her fantasy, her feelings for the child are complex and conflicting, and they will include jealousy. As we have seen, stepmothers set out expecting to love their stepchildren at once, and are appalled when they discover in themselves feelings of resentment, antipathy and, at times, even hatred instead of affection. And the antipathy may spring from jealousy – jealousy of the bond between the father and child, and jealousy of the sexual relationship which previously existed between the father and another woman. Adoptive mothers may harbour feelings of jealousy towards their child's birth mother; foster mothers may be jealous of the loyalty of their foster child to his or her own parents. In both these instances, the jealousy arises out of feelings of affection for the child, who is the first concern, and is not jealousy *of* the child, of the child's right to the love of the father. The degree to which this applies to every stepmother will, of course, vary widely as will the length of time the jealousy lasts. The point is that, in order to create a bond of affection with a stepchild, the stepmother will have to overcome powerful feelings within herself and at the same time cope with a lack of social approval. The wonderful thing is that most stepmothers manage to do this. It takes at least four or five years – probably more – and that bond will be different in every family.

Each of the thirty women I interviewed had found her own unique way to be a positive presence in the lives of her stepchildren. It was not always to her satisfaction and was never the fantasy she had had in the beginning. In two instances where the couple's relationship had ended, the stepmothers were amazed, and deeply touched, to discover that the stepchild held onto an attachment with the stepmother and wanted it to continue. In both cases the relationship between them had been fraught with difficulties for several years, and in one, disagreements over handling the child had been the most important factor in the failure of the marriage. But even several years after it had ended, the stepdaughter kept in contact with her stepmother and wanted her to be involved in important decisions and events in her life. In the other example, the delayed expression of attachment and affection between stepmother and stepdaughter occurred at a time of ritual – the stepdaughter's wedding.

The form this bond of attachment between stepmother and stepchild takes will, of course, depend on such practical issues as whether the two live together or meet only when the child visits the father, on how much physical care the child needs, and obviously on the amount of influence exerted by the child's biological mother. The child's age and maturity (or lack of it), the stage relationships have reached in the first family when it ended and the stage the stepmother has reached in her own life development will all play their part, as will the stepmother's personal qualities – her interests, style and personality.

One stepmother, now also a mother, talked about how she learned to make stepmothering work for herself, her husband and her stepdaughter. The pattern of access was weekend visits and some holidays, with some weekends set aside for the father and daughter without the stepmother being present. She said she had

'learned lessons on the way. I didn't know what being a parent meant [at first]. . .I felt like a guest for a long time. . . .Now

visits are a mixture of some which include me and some. . .just the two of them. I realised that was important – that I shouldn't always be there, but that the sort of time they had been used to should continue for some visits. Also, I found the time alone good for me, and after pregnancy especially. The times between her visits here seem to go by very quickly. . . .She is a lovely person. . .and there's more to it, something I have found out since, which is that I can explore my own girlhood through her. I get a sense of excitement out of doing things with her that I did when I was her age. I sort of know what she will enjoy doing next, and so far I have been right. It's good, a good relationship. . . .I am another adult to look out for her, another person to share things with. She is another person to share things with for me too – my recollections, pursuits, explorations, I share with her. . . .My advice? Enjoy it! [But first] create your own place. Don't try to substitute, don't enter into disciplining if someone else is already doing it – but don't stand for any nonsense!'

Here is another part-time stepmother:

'I remember what a big step it was for me to brush her hair. . . .I still don't know how to cope when [she] is ill; that's a kind of intimacy, and one she has with her father, who is very good with her when she's ill. He can let her regress and did when she was coping with all the changes. I used to get embarrassed. . . .It sounds smug, [but] now I think I bring more ideas into her life. She copies me, and hears about more that women are, or can be, from me. . . .[And] I think it's helpful to her that another woman loves [her father]. I am a bridge for her in lots of ways.'

A full-time stepmother, with two stepsons whose mother died when they were in mid-childhood, has this to say:

'I have had far more to do with [my stepsons] than I ever intended. At first, I was surprised and bewildered by how much was expected of me. . .my husband had been bringing up the children on his own. . .but it seemed as if all the parenting responsibilities became mine. . . .I think I am seen by them as a replacement mother. They have expectations of the practical things which I provide, [some of] which, in fact, their own mother could not have done for them. . .they enjoy the benefits of this [e.g., extra income for the family]. They know that I would help them when I can and be "on their side". . . .I was advised [in the beginning] not to expect to love my husband's children. This saved me from having too high hopes and expectations at the start, and, I think, was good advice. . . .I would further advise that the woman has to work out the relationship she has with each child for herself.'

As another stepmother aptly said: 'You take on more than you can ever envisage.'

Differentness does not disappear, but over time it loses its significance, its power to hurt and divide. The steprelationship fades into the background and what people concentrate on is the importance they have for one another in the business of living.

> 'I sometimes forget, you know, now. It is all so long ago and they are all involved in their own lives. Now my daughter is involved with a man who has children. She knows their mother and they get on well and can talk about the children's welfare – *they share that concern.* [Italics mine.] And she knows I've been through all that.'

Another stepmother with many years experience said, 'For children, the worst thing must be feeling unwanted. They want to be part of a family – a steady, warm background. A stepmother can certainly provide that.' A stepmother who never had children of her own and is now a stepgrandmother wrote a long description of her experience after hearing a radio interview about stepfamilies; she concludes that differentness matters and must be respected – then it can be accepted.

CONCLUSION

The worth of a stepmother

Your beautiful rays,
may they color our faces;
somewhere at an old age
we shall fall asleep old women.

Hopi woman's prayer to the sun

Writers of both professional literature and popular works leave some obvious gaps in their presentation of stepmothers. In professional articles, the stepmother is more criticised than the stepfather, and hers is described as the more difficult job. The general theme of the professional literature is that stepfamily life is full of problems; studies which focus on the pitfalls neglect the strengths and satisfactions to be found. That gap is narrowing a little with, for example, Papernow's work (1984) on the stages of development a stepfamily goes through, and that of Knaub and her colleagues (1984), who have examined how members of stepfamilies themselves perceive their family's strengths. There is a need for more work on stepmothers, on how they perceive the rewards as well as the strains of stepmothering. In my experience – in my personal experience and in my work with stepmothers – the understanding of certain other people is of vital importance. I do not mean commiserating understanding, but acceptance by, and approval of, the stepfamily itself. I note that Knaub and her colleagues found that an important predictor affecting the families in their study, affecting their positive adjustment, was the attitude of others in the environment – friends, family and the community in general. In other words, the opinion of the family others hold and convey has an impact on the opinion the family holds of itself. The stepfamily is one of several family forms; it is not a deviant form, nor sub-standard, nor is it disabled or somehow handicapped in a world of otherwise 'normal' families. It is important to understand the issues in stepfamilies and not to assume that the family is disadvantaged and it follows that it is also important to understand and value what stepmothers do.

Popular literature is a part of the social environment; it serves, among other things, to express attitudes and beliefs, and is one of the most important channels for the transmission of cultural messages. As we have seen, stepmothers in popular literature tend either to be terrible – a curse to children – or surrounded by a saintly glow. It is interesting to note that women rarely seem to write about stepmothers, though they frequently write about mothers. Two collections of short stories (Koppelman, 1985; Park and Heaton, 1987), a total of forty-three, all by women writers and all about mothers and daughters, contain only two about stepmothers. This is striking, since we might assume that a number of the writers would either be stepmothers them- selves, or have had a stepmother. The relationship between a mother and a daughter is a subject women writers return to throughout their writing careers (Koppelman) but, on the evidence in these two collections, they do not write about the classic stepmother or about any stepmother at all with the frequency we might expect. There are stories about mothers and daughters who are close and loving, about hatred between them, about weak or unreliable mothers, about daughters asking for stability and certainty, about the search for identity and approval, about oppression and disadvantage, but none about cruel stepmothers. In the two stories where the mother figure is a stepmother, she is depicted as being concerned in a loving way about a stepdaughter's well-being and self-respect in a world which threatens it. This is equally true of other substitute mothers in the collections, women such as grand- mothers, aunts, or older friends, who choose to act as mothers. Koppelman writes in the introduction to her collection: 'None of the surrogate mothers represented in this collection wonders for a moment whether she is more the "real" mother than the biological mother. She simply relates to the younger female in ways that we immediately recognize as "mothering" ' (Koppel- man, 1985, p. xxx). That is, she protects, comforts, plans, guides, feeds, entertains and worries. Women writing short stories for women to read seem to be less concerned about the

significance of biological connection than about what daughters
need from mothers or mother substitutes. Every woman looks
to older women for a blueprint for living in a world where
women are very often devalued, for understanding and for
nurturance in the process of growing older, for direction in
establishing self-respect and independence. When the older
woman is a stepmother, as far as the stories in these collections
are concerned, what is important about her is her concern for
the younger woman.

All forty-three stories are written from the perspective of the
daughter. Mothers are portrayed with sensitivity; daughters
know what mothers have to do and how difficult their task is,
but the predominant theme is what daughters need from
mothers. If these stories had been written from the mother's
perspective, the emphasis would obviously have shifted, perhaps
to the loss of the closeness that comes when a daughter grows
up, or to the criticism a daughter levels at her mother as she
begins to assess herself in the adult world and, by implication,
her mother. If these stories had been written from the
stepmother's perspective, there would surely have been yet
other differences. Because the stepmother only rarely experiences the unity with a tiny girl which a birth mother or an
adoptive mother experiences, that theme would have little
emphasis, unless perhaps the very absence of early closeness
were the focus of a story. I think stories by stepmothers might
be about the child's power to confirm or deny the stepmother's
right to have a place in the child's life, or about the way folk
tales can shape the stepmother's experience. They might
describe the fear of rejection. There might be stories about
confronting feelings of hatred towards a child, and I can imagine
a fantasy story in which a stepmother metamorphoses into the
ugly creature in fairy stories when she recognises she has such
feelings. There might be moving stories of self-sacrifice, and
overblown sentimental stories. Lurking behind them all would
be the negative images of stepmothers, images which do not
seem to lurk behind the stories about stepmothers when written
from the daughter's perspective.

Scholars have begun to explore the social influences of fairy
tales. These stories present social relations, moral codes and
prescribed ways of behaving. Once fairy tales became available

as literature they began to play a part in setting and maintaining norms. The area in which they have been most influential is that relating to traditional values about male and female behaviour. Feminist critics (e.g. Dworkin, 1974) emphasise, in particular, the oppressive effect they have had on social and cultural standards for feminine behaviour. In fairy tales, the highly valued women are passive and compliant; they do not make decisions or take actions, they are protected by men or by magic. They are often asleep or dead! In contrast, the active women are destructive and evil. Those who criticise the way women are portrayed in fairy tales call attention to issues of power and control and cite the example of the stereotyped stepmother: she is always evil, therefore powerful. The child – always good, passive and beautiful – is powerless; she has to be rescued by a prince or other strong male. These scholars and critics point out that there is another tradition in folk tales in the Western World, one in which women appear as aggressive and active and are honoured for it; but this tradition has been suppressed in contemporary literature. The strong, active females – goddesses – of the original oral tales in circulation since before the Middle Ages, were gradually transformed into witches, evil fairies, or stepmothers (Zipes, 1988), the apparition which hangs over the lives of modern stepmothers. Few people are even aware of this original tradition (Zipes, 1986). As far as I know examples of the ancient tales featuring independent and active women have not been made available in modern editions, although an effort has been made to rewrite tales, or to create new ones which present different images of both men and women. Some of these are criticised for making the male characters one-dimensional and biased (Zipes, 1986). It is no solution to reverse the bias in favour of female characters, but I was dismayed to find that some of the rewritten fairy tales still contain the stereotyped stepmother. For example, *The Moon Ribbon* by Jane Yolan in a collection of modern fairy tales (Zipes, 1986) is a revision of *The Tale of Cinderella*. In Yolan's story the child gains strength, as well as advantage, from a female figure and through magic; she is not rescued by a male figure. She takes her own action to change the situation in which she is being abused, but her abuser is the same old wicked stepmother. If, as Zipes points out, feminist writers try to suggest alternatives to the traditional sex roles in fairy tales by writing stories in which both males and females have choices and do not dominate each other by means of gender, could they not have found an alternative for the wicked stepmother? As the numbers of real-life stepmothers increase and forms of step-mothering become more diverse, so the need to find alternatives to the existing stereotype of the stepmother also increases.

Stories about stepmothers, or stories in which a stepmother figures, might be about change and getting used to change, and about different people who are important to children in different ways. One of the advantages of stepmothers – and stepfathers too – is that they provide additional sources of identification for children, another adult role model, and often, as we have seen, another adult in whom to confide and trust. Stepparents relate to the child with less intensity than birth or adoptive parents, and this can benefit parents as well as child. Children need an intense relationship with parents, but stepparents have a value also. I have not seen a revision of *The Story of Cinderella* in which the stepmother helps the child to accept the loss of her mother, and does it without asking the child to cease loving the dead mother. Yet this is exactly what many stepmothers do.

I came across a book of modern stories for children which includes one about a stepmother, called simply *Stepmother*. The little girl in the story has a stepmother because her own mother has died. The stepmother puts no pressure on her little stepdaughter to accept her, but instead creates an atmosphere in which the child can decide when to make an approach (Mahy, 1986). The stepmother is very good, very pretty and patient, and obviously very wise; perhaps, therefore, she is not altogether plausible. That aside, the story is refreshing because it begins, unlike the fairy stories, with the child's resentment and the child's power to exclude, and makes those feelings under-standable. Fairy tale stepmothers provide an important context for the story; the little girl expects the stepmother to be wicked because she imagines that is what stepmothers are supposed to be like. The stepmother shows her that her expectations were wrong and even teases gently: 'In fact, I'm feeling rather wicked at the moment. Run away quickly before I dress you in rags and make you do all the housework.'

We know that stepmothers have to overcome negative

expectations, that these arise from the lack of positive images of stepmothering as well as from their own lack of certainty about how to be a stepmother. Parenting is learned almost entirely through the experience of having been parented, that is, from one's own parents. For a stepmother, an acceptable role model hardly exists. We know that women who are confident in other areas of their lives lose confidence as stepmothers and often, in that part of their lives, feel a sense of failure and worthlessness. A stepgrandmother wrote these thoughts, looking back over many years and remembering what it had been like for her:

> Your life is particularly difficult in that you have arrived in the middle of a complex situation without happy, early memories to sustain you. . . . You cannot slip easily into the attitudes of an established marriage and family life. The love and loyalty [your partner] and his children have for each other can easily be used to isolate you, keeping you the out-sider. Even subconsciously, he may see you as the 'wicked stepmother', and in any dispute spring to [the children's] defence, thus making your job much more difficult and even impossible. (unpublished)

This woman counsels stepmothers to maintain outside interests and friends in order to enhance the sense of being valued, of having a value to oneself and others; she warns that members of the wider family may devalue the stepmother and treat her as an outsider.

Stepmothers have so much to learn and to overcome, it is incredible that any manage to do it. Yet, the stepmother I have just quoted has survived, and enjoys the family life she now has, sharing friendship and affection with grown up stepchildren and a deep relationship of mutual respect with her partner. She is fortunate. Not every stepmother succeeds, and those who do receive little publicity, while the unsuccessful stepmothers are remembered all too clearly, and are cited as confirmation of the wicked stepmother myth. For example, a twenty-five-year-old woman taking part in a television series about psychotherapy became distressed at the mention of her stepmother. When the therapist commented on her distress she said, 'I'm upset because she took my father from me.' She went on to say that her stepmother 'wouldn't let us be what we were meant to be' and that she had disliked her stepmother 'from the start'. The therapist said she seemed almost to be talking about her 'wicked stepmother', to which the girl responded: 'Yes, it is like that.'

The therapist then asked her, 'When were you cut off from your natural mother?' (Channel 4 series *A Change of Mind*, 21.11.86).

The therapist's discussion of the interview pointed out that the stepmother had become the focus of anger and bad feelings because it is safer to be angry with a stepparent than with natural parents. This is a process in which all stepmothers become involved. The first reaction to a stepmother is anger – anger that she is there at all – and it is safer to be angry with a substitute, a stranger, than with a mother who died or left, or somehow failed to prevent the painful change from taking place. Children need approval from their parents; it is linked in an essential way to finding approval for oneself. Very often, in the first encounters with a stepmother she is not approving. She enters and starts criticising; she finds a complicated scene in which she has an ill-defined role to play so she tries to change it quickly, for which she is understandably resented.

Mothers are important and irreplaceable. Because it is the mother who cares for the child first of all, and because our society depends upon mothers to care for children, they are more central to children and to family life than fathers. Fathers are important, of course, and when directly involved in the daily care of young children their significance for those children increases. Society expects, however, that the mother will look after children and, thus, she will dominate their earliest memories. To lose her is to lose a part of oneself.

A sample of 400 young adults were asked to assess their parents and family life. By and large, they said that their mothers had been more successful as parents than their fathers, but not so the stepmothers. Although less than half of those in a stepfamily described it as an unsatisfactory family, those people tended to be more negative about stepmothers than stepfathers. There were some admired stepmothers, however (Slater and Woodside, 1951). As this sample was taken before the steep rise in the divorce rate, it is no surprise that all the parents had been lost through death or permanent separation. Approximately 26 per cent had lost a parent before the age of 14, and 10 per cent of those had lost a mother. Many of the fathers would have died during World War II. Since this study was made the divorce rate has increased and there has been a proliferation of studies into the effects of divorce on children, followed in turn by research into stepfamilies. I have drawn on some of the findings of recent research when preparing this book. Do children in contemporary studies of stepfamilies make the same negative assessment of stepmothers as those in Slater and Woodside's 1951 sample?

Adolescents living in stepfamilies were asked by a researcher to assess how much stress they experienced in their families. They were asked about such matters as discipline, divided loyalties, wanting their natural parents to reunite and living in two households. There were eleven items in all, 103 adolescents, with an age range of 12–18 (Lutz, 1983). The number with stepmothers in this sample was small. Even so, the results provide some indications, one of which is that the stepdaughters with stepmothers found the relationship more stressful than did stepsons with stepmothers. However, girls with stepfathers also found the situation more stressful than did the boys. In this sample at least, girls suffer from a higher level of stress in stepfamilies than do boys, and a higher level was shown for stepmothers than stepfathers. However, there are other results to note from this research, namely, which issues these young people found most stressful in their stepfamilies. The highest level of stress was caused by divided loyalty and was most acutely felt when one natural parent spoke negatively about the other natural parent. I can support this finding from personal experience and from my contacts with stepchildren in my work as a family therapist. To hear an absent parent criticised by the other parent, possibly in conversation with a stepparent, is to feel torn apart. Children are the product of two parents and take criticism of the absent parent as a condemnation of themselves (Visher and Visher, 1979).

The second most stressful item was discipline, an area which is stressful for all families when the children are adolescent and at a stage in their development when it is normal to rebel and challenge authority. Eighty per cent of the adolescents in this study found particular difficulty in accepting rules and punishment from a stepparent. However, the longer the stepfamily had been in existence, the less of a problem the issue became. Again, the Vishers provide insight. They say that rules, expectations and punishments from an adult work only when the recipient of the discipline actually cares about, and wants approval from, the adult. It takes time for a caring relationship to develop; there must be good experiences for trust to grow. When the stepchild has experienced the positive regard of the stepparent it will begin to matter when that stepparent is disapproving. Positive regard is not to be confused with instant love. It means respect for the child's previous family experience and ties, and concern for the child's quality of life – safety, comfort and well-being. It is different from the deep sense of responsibility and affection people usually feel for children they have from birth, but it is no less necessary to the child.

In Lutz's study, the matter which caused least stress to the adolescents had to do with being a member of two households and with attitudes towards their stepfamily when they had to explain it to others. Almost 90 per cent said they had had to explain the nature of their family, but only 27 per cent had found this stressful to do. As to living in two households, most of these adolescents did not find the adjustments difficult to make; what was a source of unhappiness was *not* being in contact with both their parents. Lutz concludes that having children move back and forth between two households is more difficult for the adults to adjust to than for the children. It is hard to share children – so hard that one parent often gives up or is cut off, and that is what the children find deeply painful.

A point to note from this study is that the mean score for all the subjects was not high and was lower for those who had lived in stepfamilies for two or more years. The score would not have been as high as it was had a different method of scoring been used. Items which the respondents marked 'does not apply', that is, items which were not stressful for those individuals, were not computed. If they had been, the level of stress for this sample would have been less (Ganong and Coleman, 1984). Lutz comments:

> Generally speaking, it may be that stepfamily life is not as stressful as the literature suggests. Perhaps after the initial period of adjustment, the stepfamily milieu is not decidedly different from other family systems in relation to stress.
>
> (Lutz, 1983 p. 375)

If stepfamily life becomes less stressful for adolescents after two or more years, it is logical to assume that the same is true for the adults. However, this may not apply to stepmothers, for whom the difficulties are more deep-seated and complex. They have to contend not only with day-to-day matters, but with the question of whether they are being successful or unsuccessful in their role. Lutz does not deny that the stepmother's role is more difficult, and more stressful, than the stepfather's, although the evidence in this study does no more than indicate that stepmothers have a more complex role to fulfil. There is much in this study, however, to encourage and to guide stepmothers and others who are concerned.

One final point: it is generally assumed – as has been previously mentioned – that stepfamilies which are formed following the death of a parent are easier to establish than those which are formed following divorce. Lutz did not confirm this. She found that the stress score was higher for adolescents in a stepfamily formed after the death of a parent than for those whose parents had divorced. She speculates that adults may adjust more easily to stepfamily life following bereavement than do children and that they translate this into the belief that the children are adjusting in the same way. My personal experience, in a stepfamily in which one partner was divorced and the other widowed, is that it is more difficult to establish a trusting relationship with a child is who grieving than with one whose parent is still living. The safe generalisations, however, are that it takes time, that the stepparent must not immediately assume a disciplining role, and that the stepmother will have more difficulty in relating to stepchildren than will stepfathers. More is expected of a woman; it is she who regulates the emotional life of the family; it is hard for her to hold back, to wait for time to be her ally, to relinquish most of the disciplining to her partner during the first year or two.

The most important lesson to learn from stepchildren about stepfamily life is that they value their families and take pride in their family identity, even though they do not deny that there are problems in stepfamily living (Knaub and Hanna, 1984). A supportive environment, a sense of belonging and of being accepted is what children want and need. Stepmothers, in all their permutations, play a huge role in providing this, and they should be valued for it. They need to have a more positive attitude towards themselves and the job they do as stepmothers, and this is linked, obviously, to social attitudes. I have found that, even when a stepmother can point to success in her stepfamily, her stepmother status is not a matter of personal pride. The ideal of the nuclear family is too deeply ingrained. But the children, it seems, are proud of their family when they feel they belong to it, whatever label it has.

One of the most significant contributions many stepmothers make to the lives of their stepchildren is to ensure the children do not lose touch with their mother. Several of the stepmothers I spoke to, like this one, do this, even when it causes them pain.

> **'They care about their mother and they always will care about her, but there is the part of you that deeply resents that. . . because of all the daily things you have done, cared for them and about them. . . .I push them to write to her, to remember her birthday and things like that. I encourage them to think of her in positive ways – not just extra money for Christmas. . . . And under all that, there is the fear of losing them.'**

The natural mother in this instance left the children in their father's care. The stepmother is a full-time one, and now has a child of her own. She knows what she can and does give her stepchildren, but she continues to wonder whether it is enough, or whether her relationship to her stepchildren is secure.

Burgoyne and Clark (1984) found that some stepmothers do realise there are certain advantages in stepfamilies for children, and recognise their contribution in enhancing those advantages. Burgoyne and Clark write:

> Where parents had themselves come to terms with those aspects of their family life and relationship which prevented them from behaving as a completely 'ordinary' family they were more likely to talk about these as potential advantages rather than as hindrances to their passing as an unbroken family. . . .[One stepmother] had taken great pains to ensure that her husband and stepchildren did not lose touch with his first wife's family so that the children now have, 'a wider. . .a larger family. . .they've got my side as well and I've kept the whole family together. . . .I don't think they've lost out on anything, in fact I think possibly they've gained.' (p. 184)

Ganong and Coleman (1984) reviewed thirty-eight empirical studies of the effects of remarriage on children. These studies, published between 1956 and 1983 do not take a gloomy view or make dire predictions for stepchildren, although the data from them are too fragmented and incomplete to be conclusive. Study samples tend to be small, and until there are studies which have been carried out over long periods of time it remains unsafe to make predictions on every facet of every stepfamily situation. Before society's attitudes will change or social policies reflect a more positive view of stepfamilies, more research will have to be carried out, research which takes into account many complex factors. There are many types of stepfamilies, many variations as to ages; gender of children in relation to stepparent must be considered and gender of stepsiblings in relation to each other, along with other factors, such as influences from outside the family which have an impact on family integration. Poverty, race, class, or familial prejudices, family history, attitudes of the extended family towards the stepfamily – all are significant. Moreover, as Ganong and Coleman point out, research on stepchildren has taken a 'deficit-comparison' approach; researchers assumed that stepfamilies, because they varied from the nuclear family, were unable to provide enough emotional and psychological care for children, and they formulated questions from that perspective.

In another study, apparently completed after the 1984 survey was published, Knaub and Hanna (1984) reported their work on children in stepfamilies. It is not based on comparisons with the nuclear family, but is focused on the children's perceptions of family strengths in their stepfamily – what is there, rather than what is missing. The findings showed that the sample of forty-four children rated their families in positive ways. There is seldom enough research to provide final answers, but these researchers are sufficiently confident in their findings to warn the helping professions, and the wider community, that they must respect children's pride in their families and not imply that stepfamilies are inferior or pathological, or that children are disadvantaged simply by belonging to them.

The question we must confront here is: to what extent is a woman disadvantaged by being a stepmother? Most of those I spoke to, if not all, said that they were disadvantaged in many ways, whether or not their satisfaction in relation to a partner is high. The partnerships of two of the thirty women have ended and one was close to ending. All three blamed the failure of their marriage on conflicts concerning the children. Another woman is now in her second marriage as a stepmother, the first having given way under the strain. In three of these four instances the stepfamily type was a 'combination' (Robinson, 1980), meaning that both partners had previously had children. A number of questions arise: for example, will the stepmother who has children of her own be subjected to pressures and conflicts if she mothers the different children differently? Is a woman in a 'combination' stepfamily more disadvantaged than a woman with no children of her own? On the other hand, women with no children of their own feel disadvantaged by their own lack of experience, and undervalued by people outside the family who seem to automatically assume that such a woman has nothing positive to offer a stepchild. Some, who have since had children, talked about the unrealistic expectations they had had in the early days, caused in part by their lack of knowledge about children. However, twenty-seven of the thirty women I talked to, or corresponded with, said that they had a good relationship with their partner in spite of their distress and self-doubts as a stepmother. Some had been in a partnership, and therefore had been stepmothers, for a very long time, two of them for over thirty years. At times, they still struggled with a sense of having been a failure as a stepmother, either because their feelings for their stepchildren were not the same as their feelings for their own, or because they blamed themselves for troubles the stepchildren experienced in their adult lives. A mother's success is hard to weigh up and no mother feels she did all the right things, or enough of the right things, for her children. Success in stepmothering may be impossible to assess, since it is compared to an impossible ideal. Women as mothers face many conflicts and problems, but their reward is universal, social approval, even sanctification. The stepmother has no public reward, hers will be private satisfaction. She may find pleasure in her stepchildren in time, and enjoy her relationship with her partner; she will certainly have the understanding of another stepmother. If others in her social world, her relatives and friends, have a positive attitude towards her as a stepmother, her strength and sense of satisfaction in her role will increase.

Family shape and structure are varied and changing. Step-families and families headed by one parent will together probably outnumber first families in a few years. This is predicted for the USA by 1990 (Visher, 1984). Furthermore, many adults choose to remain single and some live in stable unions which do not appear as families in household surveys, whether they are both parents or a parent and stepparent. But they are families and they are part of the community; their children attend schools, they use the health services, they contribute to the life of the society just as any family does. The traditional family, consisting of a couple never before married, the man the sole wage earner, the woman at home full time, and two children, is a minority group (Henwood, *et al.*, 1987). In spite of the dwindling number which conform to it, this is still the prevailing norm and the type of family featured in commercial advertising. Families with structures which do not fit the norm, those I have referred to and others as well, our culture deems deviant. Changes in attitude towards the family and what it should be have lagged behind changes in the way many people are actually living.

If legislation is an indication of changing attitudes, then there are signs that social attitudes towards divorce and towards stepfamilies at least are becoming more tolerant. Society has sanctioned divorce by passing laws which make it simpler and less expensive. Counselling divorcing couples has developed into the conciliation movement and an accepted part of the work of many social agencies. The Children Bill (1988), not yet law at the time of writing, seems to demonstrate that attitudes towards stepparents are moving towards greater acceptance. The Bill is based on the principle of the rights of children, rather than the rights of parents and those holding parental status; the emphasis is on the responsibility of parents in meeting children's rights. The Bill recognises children's right to remain in contact with both their natural parents, but also recognises the importance of other parent figures. Under present law, stepparents can be held responsible for the financial support of a child under certain circumstances, but this Bill makes it possible for a stepparent to apply for a 'residence order' or a 'contact order' by entitlement. Stepparents are not named by that title, but 'persons', distinct from parents or guardians, with whom a child has lived or who have been in a marriage which has regarded the child as part of the family, will be enabled to play an important part in a child's life under this Bill (Section 7 in Part II). 'Persons', surely, might be stepparents. It appears to be a step towards acknowledging that adults – other than biologically related ones – can be of crucial significance to children. Stepmothers and stepfathers cannot take the place of natural parents (or adoptive parents known from birth), but their importance to children might in some cases be equal to that of natural parents, and could thus constitute a ground for a child's maintaining contact. One of the stepmothers I interviewed told me of a conversation between members of her stepchildren's extended family. They were discussing what would happen in the event of the death of both the children's natural parents and she realised that they never considered her an appropriate person to provide a home and care for the children, even though she was in regular contact with them, and saw more of them than any of their relations. Under this legislation she has an acknowledged right to act on her own behalf or, more accurately, on behalf of the children.

The rest is up to stepmothers. Talking to other stepmothers helps to alleviate feelings of guilt and isolation; outside agents who have information and understanding can provide advice or counselling; partners can help by being patient, showing affection and setting the limits for the children while the stepmother builds up her own relationship with them. Having other activities and rewards helps to keep self-respect alive when family life is difficult. Without some of this a stepmother will despair and blame herself. Every stepmother has to find the meaning of stepmothering in her special family.

If the worth of stepmothers is to be recognised, if they are to be valued by society and to have value in their own eyes, there must be a new concept for the meaning of the word stepmother. The myth of the wicked stepmother must be swept away without installing the myth of the perfect mother in its place. A definition similar to that of the word godparent gives us a more accurate picture of a stepmother's worth. Think, for a change, of stepmother as a very special form of godmother, not present at baptism, but sponsoring the welfare of a child in the world in the way godmothers are enjoined to do. Godmothers are an extra, not a substitute, mother. Stepmothers are additional in a similar way. Godmothers are not obligated to have the same feelings as a mother, nor do they expect the same affection from a child. Godmothers honour the mother, while providing an additional dimension. Therefore – 'Stepmother: a sponsor to the child of one's partner.'

Postscript to the open letter

From talking to you I know that many of you are wiser than I was. I have been humbled to see the amount of love and respect you give your stepchildren while trying to find your many different ways to fulfil your role without encroaching upon the loyalty of a child to a mother. But I know that some of you have looked back over the years and that you echo my own message, 'Don't pretend; don't try to pass yourself off as a mother', because you also were caught out in the game of 'just an ordinary family'. I am not suggesting that there is a magic key to success for stepmothers and that, with the wisdom of hindsight, I have found it. I do believe that it is a mistake to assume that stepmothering is just mothering at one remove. When a woman looks after a child she does many of the things a mother does, but with a different perspective of the child, and with less intensity. That can be very good for both of them.

There is no way to make it easy. Some of you have said that it takes a tough person to be a stepmother, and I agree, but I think each woman can find her own kind of toughness. I am convinced that aiming for clarity about your role is a first step. It would have helped me to know that my feelings of anger and resentment were a normal part of me and normal in the situation, not a sign of wickedness or weakness. It would have helped me to know that there are limits to responsibility, that I was not to blame for all past sufferings, nor could I put the past right by taking on unlimited responsibility in the present. I had been conditioned, like most women, to be a mother and a 'perfect' one. I therefore made myself the emotional nerve centre for the family.

When I asked you what advice you would give another woman you all said, in different ways, that it is vitally important to care for yourself, to leave a place for your own development, work and interests. I neglected that for a time,

133

but one thing I did get right was the priority I gave my relationship with my husband. We had the energy to sustain the family because we made time for ourselves. We enjoyed each other, we had fun together, and the joy and satisfaction rubbed off on the children. Although I know the children were divided sometimes – happy with the new, but loyal to the old – there is a bond between us all which had its beginning in the trust and commitment between the two adults.

It would have made things easier if I had known that however positive the new life is, the old is not cancelled out. The family which went before had its positives too, whatever may have happened to end it. For the children, it provided their first memories, their first knowing, and no other parent figures can replace the parents who were there in the beginning. A stepparent is something else. Had I seen myself as an additional person in my stepson's life, not a substitute for his mother, I could have been more confident, prouder of my position and more sensitive in the way I dealt with all the children.

I will never know if I am right! We have the saying, 'With the benefit of hindsight. . . '. It is a benefit to press our noses against the glass of our past and gaze at what has gone by for ever, to understand what happened, why it happened or what should have been done about it. It has comforted me, while I was preparing this book, to think that what has been hindsight for me may be foresight for many of you.

Yours, with many thanks,

DS

APPENDIX 1

Useful addresses

National Stepfamily Association
72 Willesden Lane
London NW6 7TA

National Family Conciliation Council
Shaftesbury Centre
Percy Street
Swindon
SN2 2AZ

APPENDIX 2

Questionnaire

The stepmothers who responded to these questions did so in a tape-recorded interview or by letter:

1. How long have you been a stepmother? Is that the way you describe yourself?
2. Are you a part-time or full-time stepmother?
3. What are the children's ages?
4. What do the children call you?
5. What did you expect of yourself at the start?
6. How has it developed?
7. Did you and the children's father talk over what was expected of you when you first got together?
8. Are you and the children's father usually in agreement about handling the children?
9. Was it like that in the beginning?
10. Do you feel at ease as a stepmother? If so, how long did it take?
11. If not, how long do you expect it will take to feel at ease? What would help you towards feeling easier?
12. Is the children's mother still living?
13. If so, do you have contact with her?
14. And if so, what do you think she expected of you at the start?
15. If the mother has died, how old were the children when she died?
16. Is she discussed or remembered or referred to?
17. Do you have children of your own from a previous partnership? This partnership?
18. Many stepmothers say their feelings for their own children are different from their feelings for their stepchildren. Is that your experience?

19. Do your feelings cause you to worry or feel guilty?
20. Do you see yourself as a replacement for your stepchildren's mother?
21. If not, what is the relationship you have to them?
22. What advice would you give to another woman about being a stepmother?
23. If children suffer as stepchildren, what do you think the cause of their suffering is?
24. What do you think society's attitude is to stepmothers?
25. Did grandparents help or hinder the process of becoming a stepmother? (There are at least three sets involved: your parents, your partner's parents, and the children's mother's parents.)

NB: Every person who responded elaborated on these questions extensively.

Bibliography

Alexander, Mrs (pseud. A. F. Hector) (1899) *The Step-Mother*, London: F. V. White.

Anderson, J. and White, G. (1986) 'An empirical investigation of interaction and relationship patterns in functional and dysfunctional nuclear families and stepfamilies', *Family Process*, vol. 25, no. 3, pp. 407–22.

Apter, T. (1985) *Why Women Don't Have Wives: Professional success and motherhood*, London: Macmillan.

Badinter, E. (1981) *Myth of Motherhood: An historical view of the maternal instinct*, London: Souvenir Press.

Barnard, J. (1975) *The Future of Parenthood*, London: Calder & Boyers.

Basile, G. B., tr. J. E. Taylor (1848) *The Pentamerone, or the Story of Stories*, London: David Bogue.

Batchelor, J. (1987) 'Stepfamily matters: experiences, expectations and beliefs', unpublished M.Sc. dissertation, Department of Sociology, University of Surrey.

Bateson, G. (1973) *Steps to an Ecology of Mind*, St Albans: Paladin.

Bell, F. (ed.) (1927) *The Letters of Gertrude Bell*, 2 vols, London: Ernest Benn.

Belotti, E. (1975) *Little Girls*, London: Writers and Readers Publishing Co-operative Society.

Blackwood, C. (1984) *The Stepdaughter*, Harmondsworth: Penguin Books.

Bulfinch, T. (1947) *Bulfinch's Mythology*, New York: Thomas Y. Crowell.

Burchardt, N. (1987) 'Stepchildren's Memories: Myth, understanding and forgiveness', Proceedings of International Conference on Myth and History, September, 1987, St. John's College, Oxford.

Burchardt, N. (1989) 'Structure and Relationships in Stepfamilies in Early Twentieth-Century Britain', *Continuity and Change*, vol. 4, pp. 293–322.

Burgoyne, J. and Clark, D. (1984) *Making a Go of It: A study of stepfamilies in Sheffield*, London: Routledge & Kegan Paul.

Burns, C. (1987) *Stepmotherhood: How to survive without feeling frustrated, leftout or wicked*, London: Judy Piatkus.

Carter, E. and McGoldrick, M. (1980) *The Family Life Cycle*, New York: Gardner Press.

Carter, E., Papp, P., Silverstein, O. and Walters, M. (1981) *Mothers and Daughters*, Washington D.C.: The Women's Project in Family Therapy, Monograph Series vol. 1, no. 1.

Children Bill (1988) London: HMSO.

Compton-Burnett, I. (1970) *Parents and Children*, Harmondsworth: Penguin Books.

Cox, M. R. (1893) *Cinderella*, London: D. Nutt, for the Folk-Lore Society.

Dally, A. (1982) *Inventing Motherhood: The consequences of an ideal*, London: Burnett Books.

Draughon, M. (1975) 'Stepmothers' model of identification in relation to mourning in the child', *Psychological Reports*, vol. 36, pp. 183–9.

Drummond, M. (1981) *How to Survive as a Second Wife*, London: Robson Books.

Duberman, L. (1975) *Reconstituted Family: A study of remarried couples and their children*, Chicago: Nelson-Hall.

Dundes, A. (1965) *The Study of Folklore*, Englewood Cliffs, N.J.: Prentice-Hall.

Dworkin, A. (1974) *Woman Hating*, New York: E. P. Dutton.

Ephron, D. (1982) 'Notes on stepmothering', *Funny Sauce*, New York: Viking Penguin.

Fast, I. and Cain, A. C. (1966) 'The step-parent role: potential for disturbances in family functioning', *American Journal of Orthopsychiatry*, vol. 36, pp. 485–91.

Fraser, A. (1984) *The Weaker Vessel: Women's lot in seventeenth-century England*, London: Methuen.

Ganong, L. and Coleman, M. (1984) 'The effects of remarriage on children: a review of the empirical literature', *Family Relations*, vol. 33, pp. 389–406.

Gaskell, E. C. (1966) *Wives and Daughters*, London: Everyman's Library.

Goffman, E. (1963) *Stigma: Notes on the management of spoiled identity*, Englewood Cliffs, N.J.: Prentice-Hall.

Goffman, E. (1968) *Stigma*, Harmondsworth: Penguin Books.

Hannam, C. (1975) *Parents and Mentally Handicapped Children*, Harmondsworth: Penguin Books.

Henwood, M., Rimmer, L. and Wicks, M. (1987) 'Inside the Family', London: Family Policy Studies Centre.

Howard, F., 5th Earl of Carlisle (1800) *Step-Mother*, London: R. H. Evans.

Hutchinson (1955) *The Stepmother*, London: Michael Joseph.

Ihinger-Tallman, M. and Pasley, K. (1987) *Remarriage*, Newbury Park, CA.: Sage Publications, Family Studies Text Series, 7.

Jung, C. G. ed. H. Read (1959) *The Collected Works*, vol. 9, London: Routledge & Kegan Paul.

Kiernan, K. (1983) 'The Structure of Families Today: Continuity or Change?' *British Society for Population Studies: The Family Conference Papers*, London: Office of Population Censuses & Surveys, Occasional Paper 31.

Knaub, P. K., Hanna, S. L. and Stinnett, N. (1984) 'Strengths of Remarried Families', *Journal of Divorce*, vol. 7, no. 3, pp. 41–55.

Knaub, P. K. and Hanna, S. L. (1984) 'Children of remarriage: perceptions of family strengths', *Journal of Divorce*, vol. 7, no. 4, pp. 73–90.

Koppelman, S. (ed.) (1985) *Between Mothers and Daughters: Stories across a generation*, City University New York: The Feminist Press.

Laslett, P. (1965) *The World We Have Lost*, London: Methuen.

Laslett, P. (1977) *Family Life and Illicit Love in Earlier Generations*, Cambridge: Cambridge University Press.

Law Commission (1986) *150,000 Children a Year: Who Cares?*, London: HMSO.

Liddell, R. (1955) *The Novels of Ivy Compton-Burnett*, London: Gollancz.

Liddell, R. (1959) *Stepsons*, London: Longmans, Green.

Liddell, R. (1986) *Elizabeth and Ivy*, London: Peter Owen.

Lorant, S. (1954) *The Life of Abraham Lincoln*, New York: Mentor.

Lutz, P. (1983) 'The step-family: an adolescent perspective', *Family Relations*, vol. 32, no. 3, pp. 367–75.

Maddox, B. (1980) *Step-Parenting – How to Live With Other People's Children*, London: Unwin Paperbacks.

Mahy, M. (1986) 'Stepmother', *Leaf Magic and Five Other Favourites*, London: Methuen.

Messinger, L. and Hansen, J. C. (1976) *Therapy With Remarried Families*, Rockville, Md: Aspen Publication.

Miers, E. S. (1968) *That Lincoln Boy*, Cleveland, OH: World Publishing Company.

Monighan-Nourot, P., Scales, B., Van Hoorn, J. and Almy, M. (1987) *Looking at Children's Play*, Columbia University New York: Teachers College Press.

Morrison, K. and Thompson-Guppy, A. (1985) 'Cinderella's stepmother syndrome', *Canadian Journal of Psychiatry*, vol. 30, pp. 521–9.

Nadler, J. (1977) 'The psychological stress of the stepmother', *Dissertation Abstracts International*, vol. 37, p. 5367B.

Opie, I. and Opie, P. (1974) *The Classic Fairy Tales*, Oxford: Oxford University Press.

Papernow, P. L. (1984) 'The stepfamily cycle: an experiential model of stepfamily development', *Family Relations*, vol. 33, pp. 355–63.

Paley, V. G (1984) *Boys and Girls, Superheroes in the Doll Corner*, Chicago: University of Chicago Press.

Park, C. and Heaton, C. (eds) (1987) *Close Company: Stories of mothers and daughters*, London: Virago.

Parker, R. (1982) 'Family and social policy, an overview' in R. N. Rapoport, M. Fogarty and R. Rapoport, (eds) *Families in Britain*, London: Routledge & Kegan Paul.

Perrault, C. (1729) tr. *Histories, or Tales of Past Times*, London: J. Pote & R. Montagu.

Rapoport, R. N., Fogarty, M. and Rapoport, R. (eds) (1982) *Families in Britain*, London: Routledge & Kegan Paul.

Rimmer, L. (1981) *Families in Focus*, London: Family Policy Studies Centre, Occasional Paper No. 6, Study Commission on the Family.

Robinson, M. (1980) 'Step-families: a reconstituted family system', *Journal of Family Therapy*, vol. 2, no. 1, pp. 45–69.

Sackville-West, V. (1983) *All Passion Spent*, London: Virago.

Sackville-West, V. (1986) *Family History*, London: Virago.

Slater, E. and Woodside, M. (1951) *Patterns of Marriage*, London: Cassell.

Sprigge, E. (1973) *The Life of Ivy Compton-Burnett*, London: Victor Gollancz Ltd.

Stacpoole, M. (1988) *Legal Points for Stepfamilies*, Cambridge: The National Stepfamily Association, Publication No. 6.

Stapleton, R. (1664) *The Step-Mother: a Tragi-Comedy*, London: J. Streaker.

Thompson, S. (1946) *The Folktale*, New York: Dryden Press.

Thompson, S. (1957) *Motif-Index of Folk Literature*, vol. 5, Copenhagen: Rosenkilde & Bagger and Illinois: Indiana University Press.

Visher, J. (1984) 'Seven myths about stepfamilies' *Medical Aspects of Human Sexuality*, vol. 18, no. 1, pp. 1–8.

Visher, E. and Visher, J. (1979) *Stepfamilies: A guide to working with stepparents and stepchildren*, New York: Brunner/Mazel.

Voysey, M. (1975) *A Constant Burden*, London: Routledge & Kegan Paul.

Walczak, Y. and Burns, S. (1984) *Divorce: The child's point of view*, London: Harper & Row.

Walters, M. (1981) 'Rebellion: Seeds of change', *Mothers and Daughters*, Washington DC: The Women's Project in Family Therapy, Monograph Series vol. 1, no. 1.

Walters, M., Carter, B., Papp, P. and Silverstein, O. (1988) *The Invisible Web: Gender patterns in family relationships*, New York: Guilford Press.

Whelan, T. and Kelly, S. (1986) *A Hard Act to Follow: Step-parenting in Australia today*, Ringwood, Victoria: Penguin Books.

Yonge, C. M. (1889) *The Young Step-Mother*, London: Macmillan. [The 1861 edition was titled *The Young Step-Mother; Or a chronicle of mistakes.*]

Zipes, J. (1986) *Don't Bet on the Prince*, Aldershot: Gower Publishing Company and New York: Methuen.
Zipes, J. (1988) *Fairy Tales and The Art of Subversion*, New York: Methuen.

Index